MEXICAN SNACKS

★ ★ ★ ★ ★

Enjoy!

Marlena Spieler

MEXICAN SNACKS

BOTANAS, TACOS, BURRITOS, SALSAS AND MORE!

★ ★ ★ ★ ★

MARLENA SPIELER

APPLE

A QUINTET BOOK

Published by The Apple Press
6 Blundell Street
London N7 9BH

ISBN 1-85076-651-7

This book was designed and produced by
Quintet Publishing Limited
6 Blundell Street
London N7 9BH

Creative Director: Richard Dewing
Designer: Ian Hunt
Project Editor: Stefanie Foster
Editor: Barbara Croxford
Illustrator: Joanne Makin

Typeset in Great Britain by
Central Southern Typesetters, Eastbourne
Manufactured by C. H. Colour Scan Sdn. Bhd., Malaysia
Printed in Singapore by Star Standard Industries (Pte) Ltd

ACKNOWLEDGEMENTS

A warm thank you to those who sampled my recipes, enjoying the successes and good-naturedly putting up with the dishes that didn't quite make it. To my daughter Leah for her continual enthusiasm for the pleasures of the table, especially the Mexican table. To my step-daughter Gretchen, with whom I have shared many late-night carnitas quesadillas picnics; to my husband Alan McLaughlan for his stamina and creative shopping; to Peter Milne for his appreciation and delicious food ideas; to Jon Harford for his vegetarian sensibility in recipe testing; to Hoops and everyone at Outdoor Chef, where the grilled and barbecued dishes were tested on the marvellous gas barbecue.

Jerome Freeman and Sheila Hannon, Amanda Hamilton and Tim Hemmeter, Christine and Maureen Smith, Nigel and Graham, Esther Novack and John Chendo, Fiona Beckett, Kathleen Griffen, Sheila Dillon, Kamala Friedman, Sandy Waks, Trish Robinson, Michelle Schmidt, Simon Parkes, Michael Bauer, M.A. and Richard Mariner for the tortilla press,

Paula Levine for the tortillas, Jill Vaux, Vanessa Welch, Etty and Bruce Blackman, Paul Richardson, Susan Redgrave, Helene and Robin Simpson, the Wight family, Lena Gilbert and Jason Gaber all tucked in to various dishes and helped in the testing, even if they weren't aware of it at the time. Thanks to Jackie Higuera McMahan, for her company one lovely afternoon in San Francisco's Mission District. Thanks, too, to my lovely cat Freud, though having a cat who insists his food bowl is garnished with fresh coriander and accompanied by tortillas is as annoying as it is amusing.

Thanks to my parents, Caroline and Izzy Smith, Aunt Estelle and Uncle Sy Opper, and Grandmother Sophia Dubowsky who whetted my appetite for Mexican food when I was young and vulnerable to this delicious life-long addiction.

And to Stefanie Foster and Quintet Publishing for commissioning me to write this book.

CONTENTS

INTRODUCTION

Snacking in Mexico is a continual feast: wherever you are there is likely to be something utterly delicious on offer at a humble stall beckoning you almost irresistibly.

The marketplace abounds with stalls piled high with fruits and vegetables, straw baskets of sea creatures, the smells of roasting meats, stacks of warm tortillas and cazuelas (ceramic casseroles) filled with savoury stews to wrap up in them. There are chickens revolving on spits, skewers of meats suspended over hot coals, and the everpresent patting of tortillas.

Bus stations, neighbourhood corners, city parks and town squares lure and entice passers-by with their seductive aromas. It is impossible to walk by – even if you thought you weren't hungry something will inevitably catch your eye and before you know it you are offering a handful of pesos and biting into a tiny taco, a half dozen briny fresh oysters dabbed with eye-watering salsa, a stick of juicy fruit powdered with fiery chilli, or even a bowl of soup with lime and pungent green chilli. Because mealtimes in Mexico are quite formalized, with a main meal eaten at midday, and a serious progression of courses, snacking is very much the opposite. It is joyfully chaotic.

At mealtimes there are rules, both social and gastronomical; the family gathers together, and the home is a cool harbour in the storm of business, school, work, and so on. And afterwards, there is usually time for a nap, to prepare for the rigours of the rest of the day.

But when snacking, there are no rules, only delight. Eat a taco at any time, walking down the street or sitting in a park, drench it with salsa and devour it in big bites by yourself or politely nibble on it with your best friend at teatime.

Mexican snacks vary from light and vivacious to solid and quite filling. You might eat walking down the street, but you might stop in at the taqueria and sit at a ceramic tiled table, downing several late-night tacos with glasses of cooling beer, while mariachis sing and strum their guitars.

Snacks are nibbled in bars and cantinas, where the owner sets out little plates of botanas (savoury nibbles such as tiny tacos, pieces of browned chorizo), to encourage more drinking. You might go for a walk through a park and pass a stall that sells soup; suddenly you find yourself supping on a bowl of richly flavoured consommé, sparked with chillies and splashed with lots of sour lime juice. When you have finished, you are utterly refreshed.

Fresh fruit is a quintessential Mexican snack – no surprise with their abundance of luscious tropical fruits. On streets you will find stalls with large jars of rainbow coloured liquids sitting in them, sweet cooling potions of puréed fruit mixed with water and sugar (aguas de frutas). There will be blenders set up at some stalls, ready to whirl creamy drinks based on milk, rice or even masa, along with the sweet fruit.

Sometimes Mexican snacks are surprising: orange slices peppered with cayenne from the Yucatan, boiled potatoes eaten from a paper cone drenched in hot chilli salsa and lime, or grasshoppers fried to a crisp crunch (*the* snack of Oaxaca).

Salsa is an intrinsic part of snacking, since a swipe of flavourful salsa turns even a plain tortilla into a near-celestial snack. Based on chillies, salsa can wake palates that have grown lethargic from the tropical heat. Salsa is endlessly varied and can range from green to red, hot to mild, fresh tasting to smoked (such as chipotle), pickled (as in escabeche). Even fruit finds its way into salsa, as the sweetness of the fruit sugar helps balance the fire of the chilli.

The following collection of recipes is a gathering of some of my favourite Mexican snacks. They range from complex to very simple, and are all in the spirit of that vibrant food I never cease to enjoy either cooking or eating.

There are a few notes I wish to include: recipes are usually streamlined both in fat content and time demands already. For instance, the traditional fat of Mexican cuisine is lard. I prefer for health reasons to use vegetable and olive oil, therefore my recipes call for oil, and usually much less than traditional recipes. However, for those who wish to cut down further I offer suggestions and variations with many of the recipes. Fromage frais, for instance, is excellent on tostadas in place of soured cream; and many tortilla-based snacks or antojitos can be piled up with salady things, crunchy and fresh, and nearly free of fat or calories. To save time, chilli powder is often terrific in place of steeping whole dried chillies for sauces and stews. Look at the end of each recipe for such suggestions.

GLOSSARY

CHILLIES

Capsicum frutescens, otherwise known as chillies, or hot peppers, come in so wide a variety they are nearly impossible to categorize. However, there are some basic guidelines to help us with the chillies that are more easily available outside of Mexico.

WHENEVER USING CHILLIES, TAKE CARE. WASH YOUR HANDS IMMEDIATELY AFTER USING, AND DO NOT TOUCH YOUR EYES OR OTHER SENSITIVE AREAS AS THE VOLATILE OILS LINGER AND LINGER. TO PREVENT YOUR HANDS FROM BURNING FOR DAYS AFTER HANDLING CHILLIES, USE RUBBER GLOVES.

WHEN HEATING CHILLIES IN A PAN, OR WHIRLING THEM IN A BLENDER OR FOOD PROCESSOR, DO NOT INHALE OR PLACE YOUR FACE NEAR THE LID WHEN REMOVING IT. INHALING CHILLI FUMES CAN BE VERY PAINFUL AND DISTRESSING. CHILDREN ARE PARTICULARLY SUSCEPTIBLE AND SHOULD NOT BE IN THE SAME ROOM WITH FRYING CHILLIES.

Chillies come fresh or dried. Fresh they are bright and full flavoured, most often available in green, but red and sometimes yellow varieties are also found. Generally, with a few explosive exceptions, the smaller the chilli the hotter.

Tiny Thai, or bird's eye chillies are very very hot, serranos on the hotter side of medium, while the larger Kenya, or jalapeño, are hot but not impossible. The jalapeño type chillies are probably the most useful all-purpose chilli, for their pleasant flavour and bearable heat. The poblano chilli looks much like an ordinary green pepper and is on the milder side as chillies go; it is lovely for stuffing. The most widely available exception to the "small is hottest" rule is the Scots bonnet, a lantern shaped chilli in parrot-like hues of red, yellow, green and orange that is breathtakingly, aggressively hot. This is one of the most readily available of chillies, and care should be taken to acclimatize yourself to its tropical heat.

Fresh green chillies may be used raw, cooked, or roasted, then added to sauces, stews, etc.

Dried chillies come in a wide range of types such as pasilla, ancho, guajillo, puya, cascabel, and so on. These are the chillies used to make "mild chilli powder". To make your own mild chilli powder lightly toast whichever chilli you desire, then cut off stems and remove the seeds. Cut the lightly toasted chilli into small pieces and whirl in a coffee grinder until it forms a powder. Storebought mild chilli powder may be mixed with paprika and used in place of the individual chillies in sauces.

CHIPOTLE CHILLI

This is the dried, smoked jalapeño, fiery hot and scented with smoke. It is available dried or in tins "en adobo", a spicy marinade. A recipe for chipotles en adobo is in the Salsa chapter.

JALAPEÑOS EN ESCABECHE

These pickled chillies are delicious with refried beans and cheese, or tucked into any taco or torta. Widely available.

TOMATILLOS

Green husk tomatoes with a sour flavour and a crisp texture. They must be husked and blanched before using, as raw they are not so delightful as when tender and ready to be puréed into sauces. Since they add a tart accent, occasionally unsweetened gooseberries or shredded sorrel, or a big squeeze of lemon and underripe tomatoes can take their place.

NOPALES

Cactus pads, an unusual green vegetable doted on throughout Mexico. Must be peeled and blanched first to rid them of their sticky juices (much like okra). Occasionally available fresh in West Indian markets; imported from Mexico in tins. If unavailable, use blanched green beans tossed with a few drops of vinegar, onion and oregano.

SOME MEXICAN COOKING METHODS

ROASTING AND PEELING CHILLIES

Place chillies of any sort over a flame and cook, lightly charring the skin, turning until evenly charred. If using small chillies, place them in an ungreased frying pan instead or skewer them before placing on flame. When evenly and lightly charred place in a plastic bag or in the bottom of a saucepan. Seal the bag or place the lid on the pan and leave for 30–60 minutes. Remove and use a paring knife to peel off. Cut off and discard the stem and remove the seeds.

TOASTING GARLIC AND ONIONS

Place unpeeled garlic cloves in a heavy ungreased frying pan and cook over medium heat until cloves char lightly and turn soft inside; turn several times so that they cook evenly. Remove from pan. To use, squeeze from skin. Use the cooked flesh and discard the skin. Onions may be toasted by cutting them unpeeled (or peeled, as desired) in half, then placing the cut pieces on an ungreased pan and cooking over medium heat until charred. Remove and use the flesh as desired.

REHYDRATING CHILLIES

Lightly toast dried chillies by holding them over a flame or tossing them in a heavy ungreased pan over medium low heat. Place in a bowl and cover with boiling water. Let sit 30–45 minutes until chillies are soft, then either purée and sieve, or scrape away the flesh from the papery skin (which should then be discarded).

MASHING GARLIC

To extract full flavour from garlic, use a mortar and pestle; add a pinch of salt before crushing.

ROASTING TOMATOES

Place tomatoes in a baking dish and drizzle with oil and salt. Bake in a medium hot oven for 45 minutes or until they shrink and concentrate in flavour. Let cool in their juices then remove skins and squeeze to extract the flavourful juices in the skins. Discard squeezed out skins and combine with the flesh of the tomatoes and with the pan juices. Tomatoes may also be toasted, using the technique described above for onions and garlic.

CHAPTER ONE

LA TAQUERIA

★ ★ ★ ★ ★

TACOS

Tacos are corn tortillas filled with nearly anything. They can be as simple as a fresh tortilla wrapped around a piece of barbecued meat or a sprig of watercress, or they can be elaborate concoctions of complex and/or elegant mixtures. You can buy them from a street vendor or at a cafe-type restaurant specializing in tacos, a taqueria.

Tacos can be soft, that is simply a tortilla wrapped around a filling. They can be crisp: either fried then filled, or fried after they are filled. Taquitos and their two-tortilla longer version, the flauta, belong to the latter category: soft tortillas wrapped around a filling, then fastened with a cocktail stick and fried in hot oil. When making soft tacos, it is authentic to use two small tortillas. However, since purchased tortillas are larger than homemade ones, a two-tortilla taco becomes more than just a snack. I have therefore adjusted the recipes to include one tortilla per taco. If you are making your own, and they are light and thin enough, by all means use 2 tortillas per taco.

TACOS DE CORDERO

TACOS OF SAUTEED CHILLI-SEASONED LAMB, GREENS, WITH GOAT'S CHEESE

MAKES 8 TACOS

5 cloves garlic, chopped

2tbsp mild red chilli powder

2tbsp tequila (or beer or vodka)

½tsp ground cumin

salt to taste

juice of ½ orange

grated rind of ¼ orange

300–350g/10–12oz lamb chops, such as loin or shoulder, boned and diced

1–2tbsp vegetable or olive oil

8 corn tortillas

150g/5oz soft goat's cheese

handful of greens, such as purslane or shredded lettuce

large pinch of oregano, crumbled

1–2 ripe tomatoes, diced

2 spring onions, thinly sliced

1. Combine the garlic with the chilli powder, tequila, cumin, salt, orange juice and rind, and mix well to form a paste. If it is too runny, add a little extra mild chilli powder or paprika.

2. Toss the lamb in this chilli paste and coat well. Leave for at least 30 minutes.

3. Brown the lamb in a tiny amount of the oil, then set aside.

4. Warm the tortillas in a very lightly greased pan or nonstick pan with a little oil.

5. Spread the warm tortillas with the goat's cheese. Sprinkle with the oregano, then spoon on the lamb. Garnish with tomatoes, greens and spring onion. Eat straight away.

NUTRITIONAL INFORMATION				
	TOTAL FAT	SAT FAT	CHOL	ENERGY
Total	95g	59g	204mg	2222kcals/9338kJ
Per Taco	12g	7g	26mg	278kcals/1167kJ

TACOS DE MOLE

SOFT TACOS OF CHICKEN AND MOLE

This is a streamlined version of mole: a savoury chilli sauce enlivened with a hint of chocolate and ground nuts rather than the complex feast of a true mole. It is worth making your own tortillas for this as their lovely corn taste is so much more aromatic than purchased tortillas.

MAKES 8 TACOS

2tbsp pasilla chilli powder

2tbsp ancho chilli powder

2tbsp New Mexico or California chilli powder

1 litre/1¾pt chicken stock, or as needed

2tbsp paprika

2tbsp peanut butter

3–4tbsp slivered almonds

2tbsp toasted sesame seeds

1 stale tortilla, cut into small pieces

handful of raisins

25g/1oz plain chocolate

3 cloves garlic, chopped

¼tsp ground cinnamon

1 onion, chopped

2tbsp oil

pinch each oregano, cumin and cloves

2 ripe medium tomatoes, diced

8 corn tortillas

pickled jalapeños (sliced, from a jar)

225g/8–10oz cooked shredded chicken

4–6 leaves Cos lettuce, shredded

2–3 spring onions, thinly sliced

2tbsp chopped fresh coriander

1. Toast the chilli powder in a heavy ungreased frying pan until lightly changed in colour but not browned and darkened.

2. Add enough of the chicken stock to the chilli to make a paste, then purée in a blender or food processor with the peanut butter, almonds, sesame seeds, tortilla, raisins, chocolate, garlic, cinnamon and onion.

3. Heat the oil in a frying pan and add this paste to the pan, stirring and cooking for about 10 minutes. Add 450ml/16fl oz stock, the oregano, cumin, cloves and tomato.

4. Simmer for about 15 minutes, adding more stock as needed, then blend in a blender or food processor once again.

5. Taste for seasoning; set aside and keep warm.

6. Warm the chicken and set aside.

7. Make the tortillas (page 74) and keep them warm in a clean cloth. Homemade tortillas can be a little thicker than purchased ones; instead of folding over or rolling up, simply serve open-faced, like a tostada, instead of a taco.

8. Smear one side with mole, pile with chicken, then garnish with lettuce, pickled jalapeño, spring onion and coriander. Eat straight away.

NUTRITIONAL INFORMATION				
	TOTAL FAT	SAT FAT	CHOL	ENERGY
Total	162g	53g	140mg	3698kcals/15534kJ
Per Taco	20g	6.5g	17mg	462kcals/1942kJ

VARIATIONS
TIME SAVING

Mole freezes extremely well for about 2 months. Divide the recipe into four containers, each enough for about ½ chicken or four enchiladas or tacos. Chicken may be purchased roasted rather than cooked at home.

VEGETARIAN

Omit the chicken and make the mole with vegetable stock. Serve topped with fromage frais or soured cream.

TACOS DE TINGA

SPICY SHREDDED MEAT SOFT TACOS FROM PUEBLA

Tinga is a spicy mixture of long-simmered meat, shredded and browned, then seasoned with chipotle chillies and often with pieces of browned chorizo, in addition. It is the filling you will find most often in Puebla: in soft tacos, crispy ones, on top of tostadas, and served simply from cazuelas, to be eaten with tortillas, lettuce and beans.

MAKES 8 TACOS

1 onion, chopped	salt, pepper and cumin to taste
3 cloves garlic, chopped	8 corn tortillas
1tbsp olive or vegetable oil, or 2 rashers bacon, diced	3 spring onions, thinly sliced
225g/8oz fork-tender cooked meat (beef, pork or lamb), shredded	5–8 radishes, diced
	2tbsp chopped fresh coriander
225g/8oz diced tomatoes, including their juices	1 avocado, peeled and sliced
1tsp marinade from canned chipotle chilli en adobo or to taste	100–175ml/4–6fl oz soured cream
	salsa of choice

1. Lightly sauté the onion and garlic in the olive or vegetable oil or bacon. Add the meat and cook until lightly browned and slightly crispy but still moist.
2. Add the tomatoes and chipotle marinade and cook down until the liquid evaporates and the mixture is dry but succulent.
3. Season with salt, pepper and cumin.
4. Warm the tortillas, then place a spoonful of the warm meat mixture on the edge of one tortilla. Garnish with spring onion, radishes, coriander and avocado, then garnish with a dab of soured cream and salsa of choice. Roll up and keep warm; continue filling and rolling until all the tortillas are filled, then eat straight away.

NUTRITIONAL INFORMATION				
	TOTAL FAT	SAT FAT	CHOL	ENERGY
Total	77g	26g	308mg	2120kcals/8918kJ
Per Taco	10g	3g	38mg	265kcals/1115kJ

VARIATIONS

Instead of soft tortillas wrapped around the filling, prepare tortillas as for tostadas, either by frying or oven crisping. Place crisp golden tortillas on a plate, one per person, and top with warm meat filling, spring onions, radishes, coriander, avocado, soured cream and a scattering of shredded lettuce.

LOWER FAT

Cook the onions in a nonstick pan and omit all but a drop of fat from browning the meat; do the same with the tortillas. Fromage frais or yogurt may be used in place of soured cream.

TIME SAVING

Prepare a tinga using meat left over from braised meats and vegetables.

13

LA TAQUERIA

TACOS DE PESCADO CON SALSA VERDE

FISH TACOS
WITH GREEN SALSA

Fish tacos are eaten throughout Mexico, filled with whatever the generous sea has offered that day. If salsa verde is not available, serve the tacos with any other fresh, tangy salsa.

MAKES 8 TACOS

350–450g/12–16oz firm fleshed white fish, such as red snapper or cod	100ml/4fl oz fish stock
salt and pepper to taste	juice of ½ lemon or lime
¼tsp ground cumin	8 corn tortillas
¼tsp chilli powder	oil for heating tortillas
pinch oregano, crumbled	Salsa Verde, as liked (page 68)
3 cloves garlic, finely chopped or crushed	2tbsp chopped fresh coriander
	2 tbsp chopped onion

1. Combine the fish with salt, pepper, cumin, chilli, oregano, garlic and fish stock in a saucepan. Gently bring to the boil, then immediately remove from the heat and leave to cool gently.

2. When cool enough to handle, break up into bite-sized pieces and season with a squeeze of lemon juice.

3. Heat the tortillas. Stack onto a plate or into a cloth-lined basket and keep covered while you finish the rest of the tortillas.

4. To assemble the tacos: gently reheat the fish, then roll up several chunks into each warm tortilla. Sprinkle with salsa, coriander and onion as you roll them up, then serve with extra salsa for dipping.

NUTRITIONAL INFORMATION

	TOTAL FAT	SAT FAT	CHOL	ENERGY
Total	7g	0.5g	161mg	1355kcals/5749kJ
Per Taco	1g	neg	20mg	169kcals/719kJ

VARIATION
TIME SAVING

Fish tacos may be prepared using leftover simmered or poached fish. Warm gently before rolling up into tacos.

NOTE

Salsa verde, or green salsa, from a jar is fine in this dish. You can enliven it with a little cumin, chopped coriander, lime juice and garlic or onion if needed.

LOBSTER AND BEAN TACOS

Elegant lobster pairs brilliantly with the humble bean in this taco that I once ate in a beachside restaurant on a lonely stretch of land south of Ensenada.

MAKES 8 TACOS

25g/1oz butter	pinch cumin
2 cloves garlic, chopped	8 corn tortillas
the meat from 2 lobster tails or 1 whole lobster	oil for warming tortillas
squeeze of lemon or lime	1tbsp finely chopped fresh coriander or parsley
350–400g/12–14oz refried beans, warmed	fresh salsa of choice

1. Melt the butter with the garlic, taking care not to fry the garlic merely warm it through and release its aroma.

2. Warm the lobster in the garlic butter. Squeeze over the lemon or lime; set aside and keep warm.

3. Season the warmed beans with cumin; set aside and keep warm.

4. Warm the tortillas in lightly oiled pan. Spread each tortilla with beans, then with several spoonfuls of lobster. Sprinkle with coriander or parsley and add salsa to taste. Roll up and serve straight away.

NUTRITIONAL INFORMATION

	TOTAL FAT	SAT FAT	CHOL	ENERGY
Total	74g	25g	261mg	2242kcals/9464kJ
Per Taco	9g	3g	33mg	280kcals/1183kJ

VARIATION
LOWER FAT

Warm the tortillas in a nonstick pan with only a drop of oil. Omit the butter and warm the lobster over hot coals, basting once or twice with a little olive oil and lots of garlic.

TACOS DEL PESCADO A LA ENSENADA

ENSENADA FISH TACOS
WITH RED CABBAGE SALAD

Tacos of fish cooked over an open fire, topped with red cabbage salad, is a favourite of the Baja California town of Ensenada.

MAKES 8 TACOS

350–450g/12–16oz firm fleshed white fish, such as red snapper or cod

salt and pepper to taste

¼tsp ground cumin

1tsp chilli powder

¼tsp oregano, crumbled

3 cloves garlic, finely chopped or crushed

2tbsp olive oil

juice of 1½–2 limes

¼ red cabbage, thinly sliced or shredded

hot pepper sauce to taste

8 corn tortillas

½ onion, chopped

1tbsp chopped fresh coriander

fresh salsa of choice

1. Combine the fish with salt, pepper, cumin, chilli powder, half the oregano, half the garlic, 1 tablespoon of the olive oil and half the lime juice.

2. Grill or barbecue until just cooked through.

3. Combine the cabbage with the remaining oregano, garlic, olive oil and lime juice. Season with salt and hot pepper sauce to taste.

4. Warm the tortillas in a lightly greased frying pan or comal. Place some warm grilled fish in each tortilla, along with a big spoonful of the cabbage salad. Sprinkle with onion and coriander, then roll up. Serve with fresh salsa of choice on the side.

NUTRITIONAL INFORMATION				
	TOTAL FAT	SAT FAT	CHOL	ENERGY
Total	29g	3.5g	161mg	1585kcals/6696kJ
Per Taco	3.5g	0.5g	20mg	198kcals/837kJ

VARIATION
LOWER FAT

Omit the oil from both the spicy paste and cabbage salad.

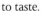

TACOS DE CAMPESINA
COUNTRYSIDE TACOS OF MARINATED AND BROWNED BEEF TONGUE

Tongue is popular in tacos all over Mexico, its smooth and firm texture and meaty taste is delicious with the other flavours of chilli, tortillas and various sauces. If tongue is not to your liking, brisket or other simmered piece of beef is delicious instead.

MAKES 8 TACOS

2 potatoes, each cut into several pieces

1 carrot, cut into pieces

handful green beans or nopale cactus

1tbsp mild vinegar

salt and pepper

350g/12oz simmered tongue (or other cut of beef, such as brisket or other roast), cut into 5mm–1cm/¼–½in thick slices

½ onion, chopped

2 cloves garlic, chopped

1tbsp paprika or mild chilli powder, such as ancho

¼–½tsp ground cumin

pinch oregano, crumbled

1–2tsp fruit vinegar or balsamic vinegar

1–2tbsp adobo marinade from canned chipotle chillies

1–2tbsp olive oil

8 corn tortillas

1. Cook the potatoes and carrot until just tender. Cook the green beans or nopales until just tender (if using canned nopales, omit this step). Allow the vegetables to cool, then peel and dice the potato and dice the carrot. Toss with the vinegar, salt and pepper, and set aside for the garnish.

2. Toss the tongue or other meat with the onion, garlic, paprika or mild chilli powder, cumin, oregano, vinegar, marinade and olive oil. Leave to marinate for 10–30 minutes.

3. Grill or pan-brown, then cut into bite-sized pieces and keep warm while you heat the tortillas.

4. Heat the tortillas then, one at a time, fill with the meat, vinegar-dressed vegetables, shredded lettuce, diced tomatoes and salsa of your choice. Serve at once, with extra salsa as desired.

NUTRITIONAL INFORMATION				
	TOTAL FAT	SAT FAT	CHOL	ENERGY
Total	100g	2g	945mg	2359kcals/9899kJ
Per Taco	12.5g	0.1g	118mg	295kcals/1237kJ

VARIATION
TIME SAVING

Omit the garnish of cooked potato, carrot and green beans. Use cooked tongue, bought at a delicatessen instead of cooking your own.

TACOS DE HUEVOS CON CARNITAS Y SALSA VERDE

SCRAMBLED EGG TACOS
WITH SHREDDED PORK AND
GREEN SALSA

Tangy green salsa is splashed onto this deliciously rich platter of scrambled egg tacos and savoury carnitas. Great for brunch or middle of the night supper, when the tequila has been flowing lavishly and the mariachis are getting ready to call it a night.

MAKES 8 TACOS

350g/12oz cooked, drained tomatillos

1 onion, chopped

2 cloves garlic, chopped

½tsp ground cumin or to taste

1 fresh hot green chilli, chopped or to taste

salt and pepper to taste

10 eggs, lightly beaten

2tbsp milk

1 spring onion, thinly sliced

25g/1oz butter or as needed to scramble the eggs

8 tortillas

350g/12oz Carnitas (page 79), or as desired, heated through

2 ripe tomatoes, diced

about 5 radishes, chopped

½–1 fresh hot green chilli, such as jalapeño, chopped

3tbsp chopped fresh coriander

1. Purée the tomatillos with half the onion and garlic. Heat through, then season with cumin, green chilli and salt. Set aside.

2. Combine the eggs with the milk and mix well. Stir in the spring onion. Scramble in the butter gently until soft curds form.

3. Warm the tortillas in a lightly oiled pan, then fill each with scrambled eggs and roll up. Keep warm while you finish rolling the tacos.

4. Surround the platter of tacos with warm carnitas, then spoon on the green salsa, with some of the tacos and meat covered with sauce, some parts uncovered.

5. Sprinkle with the diced tomatoes, radishes, chilli and coriander. Serve immediately.

NUTRITIONAL INFORMATION

	TOTAL FAT	SAT FAT	CHOL	ENERGY
Total	112g	41g	2824mg	2874kcals/12091kJ
Per Taco	14g	5g	353mg	359kcals/1511kJ

VARIATIONS
TIME SAVING

Instead of carnitas, serve the scrambled egg tacos surrounded by crisply browned thickly sliced bacon. To brown, place in a cold pan and leave to warm slowly as the fat renders: a small amount of oil may be added to the pan to coax out the bacon fat. When the bacon is browned but not crisp, place in a baking dish in the oven at 190–200°C/375–400°F/Gas Mark 6 to keep warm and crisp while the rest of the meal is cooking. Drain on absorbent kitchen paper before serving.

LOWER FAT

Instead of carnitas or bacon, use lower fat turkey or chicken spicy chorizo-like sausage. Eggs can be streamlined by decreasing the amount to 4–6 eggs and adding 225g/8oz tofu, crushed with a fork. Season with garlic and/or chopped spring onion, then cook both the egg mixture and tortillas in a nonstick pan with a few drops of oil, only for flavour. Serve tacos topped with chopped spring onions, coriander and shredded lettuce or diced tomatoes. Diced boiled potatoes tossed with roasted red and green peppers and lots of onions could be browned in a nonstick pan with a little oil to accompany the egg tacos.

TACOS POTOSINO

TACOS FROM SAN LUIS POTOSI

These tacos are filled with my favourite ingredients: light tangy cactus, rich creamy refried beans, a spoonful of smoky fiery chipotle and a few spoonfuls of whatever spicy filling I can glean from the kitchen at any given day. Spicy shredded meat, browned chorizo, diced potatoes, shellfish, sardines, even textured soya protein or sautéed tofu; any could go into a San Luis Potosi taco (though the latter two are obviously not *authentic*!).

MAKES 8 TACOS

400–450g/14–16oz Refried Beans (page 76)

1tsp ground cumin

100g/4oz mild white melting cheese, diced

400–450g/14–16oz shredded beef or pork Carnitas (page 79)

8 corn tortillas

oil for warming

1–2 marinated chipotle chillies, plus a little of their marinating adobo liquid, or as desired

175g/6oz cooked, drained nopales (canned is fine) or green beans

1tbsp chopped fresh coriander

1. Warm the beans with the cumin, several tablespoons of water and cheese. Taste for seasoning and keep warm while you prepare the other ingredients.

2. Warm your chosen filling; keep warm.

3. Heat the tortillas one at a time to make them pliable. First spray them lightly with water, then warm them in a tiny amount of oil. Stack and cover with a clean cloth while you reheat the remaining tortillas.

4. To make each taco, spread some of the warm beans across the tortilla, then a spoonful of your chosen filling. Next, add a few shreds of chipotle chilli and a drop or two of the marinade, then a spoonful or two of the cactus. Sprinkle with coriander and roll up. Eat as soon as the last taco has been rolled up, offering extra chipotle chilli on the side.

NUTRITIONAL INFORMATION				
	TOTAL FAT	SAT FAT	CHOL	ENERGY
Total	98g	31g	397mg	3012kcals/12702kJ
Per Taco	12g	4g	50mg	376kcals/1588kJ

VARIATIONS

Instead of beef filling try 1 chorizo sausage browned with 1 peeled diced potato; or about 350g/12oz peeled cooked prawns, lightly spiced with tomatoes, chillies or other savoury flavours.

TACOS MERIDA

TACOS OF MARINATED, POACHED CHICKEN
WITH ROASTED GREEN SALSA

The marinating paste is a spice paste or recado from the Yucatan: richly red with achiote and dried red chillies, fragrant with roasted onion and garlic. I like serving them with Scorched Chilli Salsa (page 69) but you can serve them with any salsa you like, tucking a few roasted green pepper strips into the tacos as you roll them up.

MAKES 8 TACOS

6 guajillo or other smooth skinned mild red chillies	1tbsp olive oil
1½ onions, toasted	½tsp salt
12–15 cloves garlic, toasted	1 tomato, chopped (canned is fine)
1tbsp ground achiote (use a coffee grinder) or whole achiote seeds soaked, cooked and pounded into a paste	3 boneless chicken breasts, cut into strips
⅛–¼tsp ground cinnamon	225ml/8fl oz chicken stock
large pinch cumin	juice of ¼ lime
large pinch black pepper	8 tortillas
small pinch ground cloves	Scorched Chilli Salsa (page 69) or 1 green pepper, roasted, peeled and cut into strips, with salsa of choice
2tbsp vinegar	
⅛tsp thyme	lettuce, cut into strips

1. Toast the chillies over an open flame, letting them catch fire a little. Do not let them burn until they are blackened, simply let them char a little more than usual and get crisp little black edges here and there. Remove from the heat and break off the stalks. Seed the chillies, then crumble the chillies into a grinder or food processor.

2. Toast onion and garlic until they are lightly charred. When cool enough to handle, dice the onion, peel the garlic, and cut up.

3. Purée the chillies with the onion, garlic, achiote, cinnamon, cumin, black pepper, cloves, vinegar, thyme, olive oil, salt and tomato.

4. Coat the chicken strips in this paste and leave to marinate for 2 hours at room temperature or overnight.

5. Bring the chicken stock to the boil, then reduce the heat to low. Add the chicken, stir through gently so that it does not break up; leave to simmer for only a minute or two. They should not be cooked through. Remove from the heat and let the warmth of the pan continue to cook them so that they cook gently and do not overcook. Just before serving, drain the chicken and toss with the lime juice. (Reserve the cooking liquid and strain for soups or sauces.)

6. Warm the tortillas in a heavy lightly oiled frying pan or comal.

7. Spoon several tablespoons of chicken into each warm tortilla. Spread with salsa, top with a handful of lettuce, then roll up and enjoy. Offer extra salsa or pickled jalapeños on the side.

NUTRITIONAL INFORMATION

	TOTAL FAT	SAT FAT	CHOL	ENERGY
Total	26g	5g	129mg	1620kcals/6860kJ
Per Taco	3g	0.5g	16mg	203kcals/857kJ

VARIATION
TIME SAVING

Omit the whole chillies and use 4 tablespoons mild red chilli powder instead. Use bought achiote paste; if unavailable, add a pinch of either grated orange rind or toasted saffron threads.

TACOS DE CAMARONES ASADERO

TACOS OF BARBECUED PRAWNS

FROM THE YUCATAN

MAKES 8 TACOS

6 cloves garlic, whole and unpeeled

3tbsp ground achiote seeds (use coffee grinder)

50ml/2fl oz grapefruit juice

50ml/2fl oz orange juice

grated rind of ¼ orange

1tsp ground cumin

1tsp ground coriander seeds

1tsp ground cinnamon

large pinch cloves or allspice

salt and black pepper to taste

2tbsp mild red chilli powder

1tbsp paprika

450g/1lb prawns, peeled and deveined

2–3tbsp oil

8 tortillas

salsa to taste

3tbsp chopped fresh coriander

Pickled Onion Rings (page 71)

1. Toast the garlic until soft and lightly charred; peel and mash. Combine with the ground achiote seeds, grapefruit and orange juice, orange rind, cumin, ground coriander, cinnamon, cloves or allspice, salt and black pepper, chilli and paprika. Toss with the prawns and leave for 30–45 minutes.

2. Thread the prawns onto skewers, then brush with oil. Grill over hot coals for 1–2 minutes on each side, or until the prawns are just turning opaque.

3. Heat the tortillas and keep warm in a clean cloth.

4. When the prawns are ready, remove from the skewers and place several into each tortilla, along with the salsa to taste and chopped coriander. Roll up tightly and serve straight away, with each taco garnished generously with pickled onions.

NUTRITIONAL INFORMATION

	TOTAL FAT	SAT FAT	CHOL	ENERGY
Total	30g	3.5g	1260mg	1742kcals/7364kJ
Per Taco	4g	0.5g	158mg	218kcals/921kJ

VARIATION

Strips of beef, pork, turkey or chicken may be used in place of the prawns.

TACOS DE RAJAS Y QUESO

SOFT TACOS OF GREEN PEPPERS, CHILLIES AND CHEESE

Rajas are simply strips of chillies; roasted, peeled and sautéed with fragrant spicing, they make a marvellous side dish, or filling for nearly anything. Here they are simmered into a creamy cheese taco filling that tastes sublime next to the delicate corn of the tortillas.

MAKES 8–12 TACOS

2 poblano or Anaheim chillies, roasted and peeled, seeded, then cut into strips

1 green pepper, roasted, peeled, seeded and cut into strips

4 cloves garlic, chopped

2tbsp vegetable oil

1½tsp cumin

1tbsp mild chilli powder, such as ancho or a New Mexico blend

1tbsp paprika

4 tomatoes, diced

225–275g/8–10oz white cheese, such as Gouda, white Cheddar, etc

1 jalapeño en escabeche, chopped

100ml/4fl oz soured cream

pinch turmeric

pinch ground ginger

juice of ½ lime or lemon

8–12 corn tortillas

1. Sauté the poblanos and green pepper with the garlic in 1 tablespoon of the oil until softened. Sprinkle with cumin for a minute or so, then stir in the chilli powder, paprika and tomatoes. Continue to cook for about 5 minutes or until tomatoes are somewhat saucelike and chunky.

2. Stir in the cheese and jalapeño en escabeche, stirring until the cheese melts, about 4–5 minutes.

3. Remove from the heat and stir in the soured cream, turmeric and ginger. Flavour with a squeeze of lime or lemon. Set aside and keep warm.

4. Warm the tortillas either by steaming or in the remaining tablespoon of oil in a heavy pan. Spoon a tablespoon or two of the melted cheese and peppers into each warm tortilla and offer extra jalapeños en escabeche as well as extra soured cream to taste.

NUTRITIONAL INFORMATION				
	TOTAL FAT	SAT FAT	CHOL	ENERGY
Total	117g	59g	285mg	2394kcals/10037kJ
Per Serving (8)	15g	7g	36mg	299kcals/1255kJ

VARIATION
LOWER FAT

Warm the tortillas in a nonstick pan. Omit the oil for sautéeing the peppers, using a nonstick pan instead. Use a low fat cheese, and fromage frais in place of soured cream.

FLAUTAS DE CAMARONES CON SALSA DE FRUTAS

PRAWN ROLLED CRISP-FRIED TACOS

WITH TROPICAL FRUIT SALSA

Finely chopped or minced prawns, strongly seasoned, and rolled up into a tortilla makes a delectable taco, especially alluring when the temperature climbs really high. Try serving these flautas in a very tropical manner, piling them onto a large banana leaf, all garnished with unsprayed edible flowers such as nasturtiums.

MAKES 8 TACOS

350g/12oz raw peeled prawns

1 onion, chopped

1 clove garlic, chopped

2tbsp chopped fresh coriander

1tsp chipotle marinade or mild chilli powder, such as ancho, or to taste

¼tsp ground cumin

⅛tsp thyme

large pinch oregano

large pinch ground cinnamon

large pinch ground cloves

1 tomato, finely chopped

juice of ½ lime or to taste

salt and pepper

8 corn tortillas

oil for warming and frying tortillas

Tropical Fruit Salsa (page 66)

1. Combine the prawns with the onion, garlic, coriander, chipotle, cumin, thyme, oregano, cinnamon, cloves, tomato, lime juice, salt and pepper

2. Warm the tortillas to soften. Place two tortillas next to each other, slightly overlapping. It will form a sort of oblong. Place several tablespoons of filling along the length of the tortillas, leaving a border around the edges. Roll up tightly and secure with a cocktail stick.

3. Fry the flautas in hot oil until lightly golden, then briefly drain on absorbent kitchen paper to blot any excess oil. Serve straight away, each flauta garnished with a spoonful of tropical fruit salsa.

NUTRITIONAL INFORMATION

	TOTAL FAT	SAT FAT	CHOL	ENERGY
Total	8.25g	0.5g	683mg	1542kcals/8090kJ
Per Taco	0.9g	neg	85mg	193kcals/1011kJ

VARIATIONS
TRADITIONAL

Spoon any tomato based salsa over the flautas, along with guacamole, soured cream and chopped onions.

LOWER FAT

Instead of frying the flautas, brush the rolled filled tortillas lightly with oil. Bake in the oven at 200°C/400°F/Gas Mark 6 until golden and crispy, about 15 minutes.

TOSTADAS

Tostadas are crisp and golden browned tortillas. Topped with a selection of varied ingredients, they are as exciting to eat as they are delicious. Each bite takes your mouth through a tour of textures: the crisp flurry of shredded lettuce or crumbling of tangy cheese, the cool billow of soured cream or the juicy nuggets of tomato, leaves of coriander or other fragrant herbs, layers of creamy beans or finely minced meats redolent of garlic and chillies. Seafood can be spooned onto tostadas, as can goat's cheese, scrambled eggs, shredded duck, as well as beef, chicken or pork, simmered shark, braised brains or grilled tongue.

Lately tostadas have become very chic in Mexico City, where they are centred in the plate, nouvelle cuisine style, topped and surrounded with various ingredients and sauces, drizzled on, painted on, treated like a canvas for the oh-so-delicious still life of toppings.

TOSTADAS POBLANO

PUEBLA STYLE TOSTADAS
WITH CHIPOTLE, SALSA VERDE AND SOURED CREAM

These crisp tostadas are topped with creamy refried beans, savoury meat or chicken, and both the tang of tomatillo and the fire of chipotle.

SERVES 4

225–350g/8–12oz leftover meat or chicken, diced or shredded

about 1tsp oil, or as needed

salt, pepper and crumbled oregano to taste

4 corn tortillas, prepared as for Tostadas (page 73)

225g/8oz refried beans (canned is fine), warmed

⅛tsp ground cumin

1 avocado, peeled, seeded and sliced

Salsa Verde (page 68) (bought is fine)

1 chipotle chilli, cut into strips

175ml/6fl oz soured cream

½ onion, finely chopped

handful of lettuce

5 radishes, diced

1. Warm the beef or chicken in the oil. Season with salt, pepper and oregano; keep warm. Crisp the tostadas, then spread with refried beans and cumin.

2. Serve straight away, topped with spoonfuls of the warm meat, avocado, salsa verde, chipotle chilli, soured cream, onion, lettuce and radish.

NUTRITIONAL INFORMATION				
	TOTAL FAT	SAT FAT	CHOL	ENERGY
Total	108g	38g	278mg	2140kcals/8970kJ
Per Serving/ Tortilla	27g	9.5g	70mg	535kcals/2243kJ

VARIATIONS
TIME SAVING

Use bought ready-roasted chicken in place of home-cooked, and canned refried beans, warmed with a little water and seasonings, as well as tomatillo salsa from a jar.

LOWER FAT

Soured cream may be replaced by fromage frais. Be sure that the meat you use is trimmed of all fat. Use a nonstick pan to brown it, without the addition of extra oil or fats.

TOSTADAS DE JICARA
CAVIAR TOSTADAS

Earthy crisp tortillas topped with luxurious, briny caviar is a provocative nibble I tasted at a Mexico City artists' reception.

SERVES 4

12 small round corn tortillas, or wedges of larger corn tortillas, prepared as for Tostadas (page 73)

175ml/6fl oz soured cream

1 small jar black caviar

1 small jar yellow or red caviar

1 small to medium onion, chopped

1. Spread the crisp tostadas with soured cream, then carefully top with black, red, and/or yellow caviar.

2. Garnish with chopped onion and serve immediately.

NUTRITIONAL INFORMATION				
	TOTAL FAT	SAT FAT	CHOL	ENERGY
Total	49g	23.5g	675mg	1356kcals/5703kJ
Per Serving/ Tortilla	12g	6g	169mg	339kcals/1426kJ

TLAYUDAS
OAXACAN TOSTADAS

Tlayudas are slightly thick, very corn-flavoured tortillas spread with various toppings for open tostada-like creations.

SERVES 4

100g/4oz cooked hominy (posole)

175ml/6fl oz cooking liquid from hominy, or water

225g/8oz masa harina

1. Blend the hominy with its cooking liquid (or water), then mix with the dry masa until it forms a thick dough, much like a child's playdough.

2. Press as for ordinary tortillas (because of its consistency, tlayudas will be thicker than ordinary tortillas).

3. Cook on a hot ungreased comal or frying pan. Stack and wrap in a clean tea towel to keep warm.

NUTRITIONAL INFORMATION				
	TOTAL FAT	SAT FAT	CHOL	ENERGY
Total	0.5g	neg	0mg	266kcals/1120kJ

TLAYUDAS ROJOS
RED CHILLI TLAYUDAS
WITH SPRING ONION BUTTER

SERVES 4

1 recipe Tlayuda (page 25)

1–2tbsp mild chilli powder, such as ancho, or to taste

100g/4oz butter, softened

3–4 spring onions, thinly sliced

1. Prepare the tlayuda but add the chilli powder to the dough.

2. Beat the butter together with the spring onions.

3. Spread the seasoned butter over the hot tlayudas and eat immediately.

NUTRITIONAL INFORMATION				
	TOTAL FAT	SAT FAT	CHOL	ENERGY
Total	83g	55g	230mg	1012kcals/4190kJ
Per Serving	21g	14g	58mg	253kcals/1048kJ

TOSTADAS DE QUESO CABRITO

GOAT'S CHEESE TOSTADAS
WITH CHILLI-GARLIC STEEPED OIL

Goat's cheese has enjoyed a great revival in Mexico in recent years. Fresh and tangy, it blends deliciously with both red and green chillies, and is so light it doesn't obscure the delicacy of the other ingredients. Though cheese from goats is traditional it had fallen out of favour with commercial cheese makers from whom the predictable, plodding cow was a dependable source of milk.

Try rolling goat's cheese into enchiladas, or crumbling a spoonful into a bowl of vegetable soup along with a handful of tortillas and salsa to taste; stir goat's cheese into migas, that dish of scrambled eggs with aromatics and totopos. Or simply roll a spoonful of goat's cheese into warm corn tortillas with a spoonful of salsa verde.

This tostada is slightly more ambitious, quite elegant with its greens, yet delightfully simple and straightforward in satisfying flavour.

SERVES 4

1 mild red chilli, such as guajillo or New Mexico, crumbled

50ml/2fl oz olive oil

1 clove garlic, cut into thin slivers

4 corn tortillas, prepared as for Tostadas (page 73)

175–225g/6–8oz goat's cheese, cut into 4 portions

sprinkling of fresh oregano or marjoram

handful greens, such as baby watercress, lettuce, purslane, lightly dressed with vinaigrette

1. Crumble the red chilli and heat together with the olive oil gently until small bubbles form around the edge of the pan. Remove from the heat and add the garlic. Leave to steep until it cools, then drain. Discard the chilli and garlic, or save them for sauce or soup.

2. Warm the tostadas on one side, then spread each with goat's cheese. Sprinkle with oregano, then heat briefly to warm the goat's cheese through. Serve straight away, drizzled with a small amount of the red chilli-garlic oil and garnished with greens.

NUTRITIONAL INFORMATION				
	TOTAL FAT	SAT FAT	CHOL	ENERGY
Total	82g	25g	0mg	1848kcals/7762kJ
Per Serving/ Tortilla	20g	6g	0mg	462kcals/1941kJ

TOSTADAS DE PATO
DUCK TOSTADAS WITH BLACK BEANS AND WILD GREENS

Another seemingly nouvelle offering that in fact goes back to traditional flavours: game meat, wild-tasting greens, and goat's or sheep's cheese. Serve with any homemade salsa for an elegant yet robust tostada.

SERVES 4

1 onion, chopped

3 cloves garlic, chopped

1–2tbsp olive or vegetable oil

salt and pepper to taste

½tsp ground cumin

3–5 tomatoes, diced (canned is fine)

meat from ½ roasted duck, cut into bite-sized pieces or shredded

large pinch mild red chilli powder, such as ancho or New Mexico

1 recipe Refried Black Beans (page 76), warmed

4 corn tortillas, prepared as for Tostadas (page 73)

about 75g/3oz crumbled fresh cheese, such as queso fresco, fresh pecorino or a not too salty feta

handful of interesting salad greens, such as watercress, arugula, purslane etc

Chipotles en Adobo (page 70), Salsa Verde (page 68) or other fresh salsa of choice

1. Lightly sauté the onion and garlic in the oil until softened. Add salt, pepper and cumin to taste, then stir in the tomatoes. Cook until a saucelike mixture forms. Set aside and keep warm.

2. Brown the meat lightly. Season with chilli powder, salt and pepper; keep warm.

3. Spread the black beans over the tostadas, then sprinkle with the cheese. Spoon on the meat, then the tomato mixture as required. Top with the salad greens and a spoonful of salsa. Serve straight away.

NUTRITIONAL INFORMATION	TOTAL FAT	SAT FAT	CHOL	ENERGY
Total	118g	34g	537mg	2519kcals/10578kJ
Per Serving/ Tortilla	30g	8g	134mg	630kcals/2645kJ

TOSTADAS DE QUESO Y GUACAMOLE
FETA AND WHITE CHEESE TOSTADAS
WITH GUACAMOLE AND SOURED CREAM

This straightforward tostada of two types of cheese, mixed with garlic and oregano then melted seductively on top, served with soured cream and guacamole, tastes sumptuous and is simple to toss together.

SERVES 4

8 tortillas, lightly oiled and crisped as for Tostadas (page 73)

100g/4oz feta cheese, crumbled

2 cloves garlic, chopped

½tsp fresh oregano or to taste

175–225g/6–8oz mozzarella or Cheddar cheese, grated

Guacamole (page 58)

175ml/6fl oz soured cream

large handful shredded Cos lettuce, lightly tossed in vinaigrette

2–3tbsp sliced pickled jalapeños

1. Arrange the tostadas on a baking sheet large enough to accommodate them (or use two).

2. Sprinkle with feta, garlic and oregano, then with grated mozzarella or Cheddar. Grill until the cheese melts.

3. Serve each tostada garnished with guacamole, soured cream and pickled jalapeños.

NUTRITIONAL INFORMATION	TOTAL FAT	SAT FAT	CHOL	ENERGY
Total	118g	63g	290mg	2399kcals/10061kJ
Per Serving/ Tortilla	15g	8g	36mg	300kcals/1258kJ

CHEESE TACOS

Simplified, quesadillas are cheese tacos. They may be little more than corn tortillas filled with cheese, then heated until it melts, or it might be fresh masa dough wrapped around cheese, then pan-browned to make a crisp cheese turnover. Quesadillas may also be made using flour tortillas. In addition to cheese, quesadillas can have any number of ingredients: salsa, chillies, sautéed meats such as brains, carnitas, or grilled meats, or savoury sautéed wild mushrooms or greens.

QUESADILLA DE CHORIZO Y ALCACHOFA
CHORIZO AND ARTICHOKE HEART QUESADILLAS

This might sound an unlikely combination, but it is a delicious variation of a cactus bud quesadilla that I have sampled. Frozen artichoke hearts are fine if fresh are not available or are too time consuming; canned artichoke hearts are acceptable if rinsed well of their canning liquid.

SERVES 4

1 chorizo, about 175g/6oz, skin removed, meat broken up

2 artichokes, trimmed of their spiky leaves and chokes, blanched until just tender (or use about 8 artichoke hearts), then diced

2 cloves garlic, chopped

4 large flour tortillas

350g/12oz mild white cheese

1 tomato, diced

2 spring onions, thinly sliced

1tbsp chopped fresh coriander

hot pepper seasoning to taste (such as Habanero or Bufala Chipotle Salsa)

1. Brown the chorizo in a dry frying pan, breaking it up as it cooks. Remove from the heat. Toss the artichokes with half the garlic.

2. Warm the tortillas so that they are pliable. Working one at a time, sprinkle each tortilla with chorizo, artichoke and cheese. Fold up to enclose the filling.

3. Heat in a lightly greased frying pan, until golden flecked and the cheese has melted.

4. Combine the tomato, spring onions, remaining garlic and the coriander. Season with hot pepper seasoning and serve a spoonful with each quesadilla.

NUTRITIONAL INFORMATION

	TOTAL FAT	SAT FAT	CHOL	ENERGY
Total	98g	59g	288mg	2068kcals/8685kJ
Per Serving	25g	15g	72mg	517kcals/2171kJ

VARIATION
LOWER FAT

Use a lower fat chicken or turkey chorizo or chillied sausage in place of the chorizo and use low fat cheese in place of full fat. Instead of rolling up the quesadilla and pan-browning, simply place the cheese side up under the grill and melt the cheese.

QUESADILLA CON CHILE VERDE Y
QUESO FRESCO DE CABRITA

GOAT'S CHEESE AND GREEN CHILLI QUESADILLAS

If your chillies are terribly piquant, place in the freezer overnight or for longer. Their heat should be somewhat mitigated when thawed. Green pepper, combined with a little smaller chilli, may be used in place of the larger mild chillies.

SERVES 4

1–2 mild green chillies (depending on heat of the chillies, 1 green pepper can substitute for one of the chillies), such as Anaheim or poblano, roasted, peeled, seeded and sliced

1 clove garlic, chopped

2tsp chopped fresh coriander

1tbsp olive oil

1tsp vinegar

pinch oregano

4 corn tortillas

150g/5oz goat's cheese, cut into slices or crumbled

175g/6oz mild cheese, grated

1. Combine the chillies with the garlic, coriander, oil, vinegar and oregano. Leave to marinate for at least 30 minutes; overnight is even better.

2. Warm the tortillas in a lightly greased heavy frying pan until pliable. Spoon the peppers onto the tortillas, then top with the goat's and mild cheeses. Fold over.

3. Heat the quesadillas in a heavy ungreased frying pan or comal until lightly browned in spots on each side and the cheese has melted. Serve immediately.

NUTRITIONAL INFORMATION				
	TOTAL FAT	SAT FAT	CHOL	ENERGY
Total	72g	41g	123mg	1362kcals/5705kJ
Per Serving	18g	10g	31mg	341kcals/1426kJ

VARIATIONS
TIME SAVING

Omit the roasted and marinated green chilli and instead use pickled jalapeños to taste. Combine with the cheeses and fill the tortillas, then warm in the comal or ungreased frying pan.

QUESADILLAS CON SALSA DE OLIVAS

CHEESE-TOPPED FLOUR TORTILLAS

WITH GREEN OLIVE AND ROASTED RED PEPPER TOPPING

This is a simple to make yet utterly delicious quesadilla. Marvellous for an any time, any weather, snack.

SERVES 4

4 flour tortillas

225–350g/8–12oz flavourful white cheese, such as white Cheddar, mozzarella, fontina, asiago, etc, coarsely grated

about 12 pimento-stuffed green olives, sliced

1 red pepper, roasted, peeled and cut into strips (from a jar is fine)

1–2 cloves garlic, chopped

2tbsp fresh chopped coriander

hot chilli sauce or salsa of choice

1. Arrange the tortillas on a baking sheet.

2. Combine the cheese with the olives, red pepper, garlic and coriander. Divide equally and make a layer on each tortilla.

3. Sprinkle with hot sauce to taste. Grill until the cheese is melted and lightly browned in spots.

4. Serve immediately, with extra hot sauce if liked.

NUTRITIONAL INFORMATION

	TOTAL FAT	SAT FAT	CHOL	ENERGY
Total	58g	31g	146mg	1595kcals/6695kJ
Per Serving	14.5g	8g	37mg	399kcals/1674kJ

QUESADILLA DE HONGOS EN TORTILLA DE HARINA

MUSHROOM QUESADILLA IN A FLOUR TORTILLA

In Mexico, the mushroom season is a parade through a rich, fungal wonderland: little brown mushrooms known as clavitos; huitlacoche, the delectable fungus that grows on corn; yemas, with their orange-yellow hue and delicate flavour; enchilados, coloured the hue of the red chilli; tecamaniles, earthy in colour and flavour; in addition to the mushrooms that Europeans and North Americans are more used to, morels and cèpes, as well as cultivated mushrooms.

I have prepared the following with an assortment of fresh mushrooms: shiitake, portobello, chanterelles, trompette de morte, and cèpes. They are also good using a combination of dried (soaked and rehydrated) mushrooms in addition to cultivated ones.

SERVES 4

225g/8oz mushrooms, thinly sliced (see above)

25g/1oz butter, plus a little extra if needed

2 cloves garlic, chopped

salt and pepper to taste

4 large flour tortillas

about 175g/6oz mild cheese, thinly sliced or grated

2tbsp chopped fresh coriander

1 recipe Salsa Cruda (page 65)

1. Sauté the mushrooms in the butter until lightly browned. Add the garlic, salt and pepper, then remove from the heat.

2. Warm the tortillas to make them pliable. Working one at a time, sprinkle each with cheese, coriander, salsa and mushrooms. Fold over to enclose the filling.

3. Heat the tortillas in a hot lightly greased pan or under the grill until the cheese melts. Serve immediately, with extra salsa if liked.

NUTRITIONAL INFORMATION

	TOTAL FAT	SAT FAT	CHOL	ENERGY
Total	60g	37g	171mg	1249kcals/5241kJ
Per Serving	15g	9g	43mg	312kcals/1310kJ

QUESADILLA CON FRIJOLES NEGROS

BLACK BEAN AND WATERCRESS QUESADILLAS
WITH CHIPOTLE CHILLI

Black beans, smoky chipotle and fresh watercress make these elegant though still earthy quesadillas.

SERVES 4

225g/8oz cooked black beans, either well spiced with garlic, onions, tomatoes and mild red chilli, or refried

2tsp marinade from canned chipotles or chipotle salsa

3–4 ripe tomatoes, chopped

2 spring onions, thinly sliced

4 large flour tortillas (30cm/12in)

350–450g/12–16oz white cheese, such as mozzarella or white Cheddar, grated

100ml/4fl oz soured cream

handful of watercress, coarsely chopped

1. Warm the beans with a few tablespoons of water so that they heat evenly and do not burn.

2. Meanwhile, combine the chipotle marinade with the tomatoes and spring onions.

3. Warm the tortillas to make them pliable. Spread them with a layer of beans and a generous sprinkling of cheese. Put on a spoonful of the tomato-chipotle mixture and fold into an envelope-like parcel.

4. Heat the tortillas in an ungreased pan, covered, or in a steamer, until the quesadilla is heated through and the cheese has melted.

5. Serve garnished with soured cream and watercress.

NUTRITIONAL INFORMATION				
	TOTAL FAT	SAT FAT	CHOL	ENERGY
Total	72g	41g	123mg	1362kcals/5705kJ
Per Serving	18g	10g	31mg	341kcals/1426kJ

VARIATION
LOWER FAT

Use low fat cheese in place of full fat, and fromage frais in place of soured cream.

BURRITOS

FLOUR-WRAPPED PARCELS

Burritos are flour tortillas filled with warm beans, savoury meats, poultry or fish, sometimes rice and/or cheese, then splashed with salsa and wrapped tightly. They are huge and unwieldy to eat, and are one of the most appetizing of dishes one can conjure up when hungry.

Any kind of beans may be used: simmered pinto or black, or refried beans. Be sure they are warm. Guacamole and soured cream may be tucked inside, as can extra salsa, chillies and handfuls of herbs. Wet burritos are basic burritos splashed with Mild Red Chilli Sauce (page 78), then sprinkled with cheese and baked until hot and bubbly. Chimichangas are burritos that are fried in hot oil until golden.

BURRITOS DE FRIJOLES NEGROS Y MOLE

BLACK BEAN BURRITOS
WITH MOLE AND ORANGE SALSA

The fruity-spicy quality of orange salsa enhances the slightly sweet mole sauce. This is a lovely vegetarian burrito, but could include any savoury braised meat, too, if liked.

SERVES 4

1 orange or 2 smaller citrus fruits, such as mandarin or satsuma, peeled, seeded and diced, including their juices and a little grated rind

1 tomato, preferably slightly unripe, diced

1 spring onion, thinly sliced

¼ onion, chopped

juice of ½ lime

½tsp sugar

1tsp hot pepper sauce from a bottle, or to taste

4 flour tortillas

1 recipe Mole from Tacos de Mole recipe (page 11)

225ml/8fl oz hot stock

1 recipe Refried Black Beans (page 76)

soured cream or fromage frais

4–5 leaves Cos lettuce, shredded or thinly sliced

3tbsp chopped fresh coriander

1. Combine the orange, tomato, spring onion, onion, lime juice, sugar and hot pepper sauce. Set aside.

2. Warm the tortillas. Simmer the mole with the stock until thickened. Working one at a time, spread a generous amount of warm beans along the centre of the tortilla, then spread generously with mole sauce.

3. Roll up, sealing in the edges first to enclose the filling, then keep warm while you finish the rest of the burritos.

4. Serve each burrito topped with soured cream or fromage frais, and a spoonful of the orange and tomato salsa. Sprinkle with lettuce and coriander and eat straight away.

NUTRITIONAL INFORMATION				
	TOTAL FAT	SAT FAT	CHOL	ENERGY
Total	129g	20g	2mg	2971kcals/12485kJ
Per Serving	32g	5g	1mg	743kcals/3121kJ

BURRITOS DE VERDERAS
BROCCOLI BURRITOS

SERVES 4

225g/8oz broccoli, diced

50g/2oz ricotta cheese, cottage cheese or fromage frais

1 clove garlic, chopped

½tsp ground cumin

100–175g/4–6oz Cheddar or asiago cheese, grated

1 egg, lightly beaten

4 flour tortillas

1tbsp vegetable oil

Chipotles en Adobo (page 70) or bought, or guajillo salsa, warmed

1. Cook the broccoli in boiling salted water until al dente, then drain. Mix with the ricotta or cottage cheese, garlic, cumin, cheese and egg.

2. Warm the tortillas in the oil until softened and pliable. Fill with the broccoli-cheese mixture, then fold over. Heat in the pan until the cheese melts and the outside of the tortilla is lightly browned in spots.

3. Serve straight away, with either the chipotle salsa or the warmed salsa guajillo. Garnish with chopped onion, chopped fresh coriander and diced tomatoes if liked.

NUTRITIONAL INFORMATION

	TOTAL FAT	SAT FAT	CHOL	ENERGY
Total	62g	29g	363mg	1271kcals/5328kJ
Per Serving	15g	7g	91mg	318kcals/1332kJ

VARIATION
WET BURRITOS

These burritos are particularly suited for making into wet burritos. Arrange one per person in a baking dish, then pour over about 350–450ml/12–16fl oz mild chilli sauce (using guajillo if liked). Sprinkle with cheese, cover with foil, then bake in the oven at 190–200°C/375–400°F/Gas Mark 5–6 until heated through. Serve straight away, with extra salsa on the side.

BURRITOS DE FRIJOLES NEGROS Y CARNE DE RES

BLACK BEAN AND BRAISED BEEF BURRITOS

WITH CHIPOTLE SALSA

Any tender, savoury beef is delicious in these burritos: use leftover braised beef, barbecued steak or prepare sautéed strips of steak or even good quality lean minced beef.

SERVES 4

½ chilli chipotle en adobo, chopped in 1–2tsp of the marinade

3–4 ripe tomatoes, diced, or canned, chopped

1 onion, chopped

1 clove garlic, chopped

1tbsp chopped fresh coriander

350g/12oz leftover chilli-braised beef, shredded, or sautéed strips of chilli seasoned beef (or use one of the fillings from page 79)

1 recipe Refried Black Beans (see page 76)

4 flour tortillas

about 2tsp oil

1. Combine the chilli with the tomatoes, onion, garlic and coriander. Set aside.

2. Shred or thinly slice the meat and warm, with a little of its flavourful braising liquid or sauce. Keep warm while you prepare the rest of the dish.

3. Warm the beans and keep warm while you heat the tortillas and assemble the dish.

4. Warm the tortillas in a little oil until pliable; fill with several spoonfuls of braised meat, warm beans and chipotle chilli tomato mixture. Roll up to enclose the filling.

NUTRITIONAL INFORMATION				
	TOTAL FAT	SAT FAT	CHOL	ENERGY
Total	128g	39g	236mg	2528kcals/10604kJ
Per Serving	32g	10g	59mg	632kcals/2651kJ

VARIATIONS
LOWER FAT

Omit the meat and fill only with beans. Use fat-free flour tortillas and serve with lots of salad and a squeeze of lime.

VEGETARIAN

Black Bean and Corn Burritos with Chipotle Salsa: In place of the beef, spoon chilli-sautéed corn into the tortillas with the beans and chipotle salsa. Add grated cheese and roll up.

To make chilli-sautéed corn: Sauté cooked sweetcorn kernels with chopped onion, garlic, cumin to taste, and either a generous shake of mild chilli powder, or a few spoonfuls of Mild Red Chilli Sauce (page 78), salt and pepper to taste.

BURRITOS DE CHILORIO
PORK AND RED CHILLI BURRITOS

The pork filling cooked with ancho chilli paste is good not only in burritos, but in tacos, tostadas, tortas and tamales as well.

SERVES 4

1kg/2lb shoulder of pork, cut into 2.5–5cm/1–2in cubes	salt and pepper to taste
5 ancho chillies	4 large flour tortillas
8 cloves garlic, chopped	Frijoles de Olla (simmered pinto beans, warmed and drained) (page 77)
¼tsp oregano, crumbled	
½tsp ground cumin	4tbsp chopped onion
75ml/3fl oz stock	salsa to taste
juice of ½ lime	Guacamole (page 58)

1. Cover the pork with water and simmer over a low heat for 1 hour or until the water has evaporated and meat has lightly browned.

2. Remove from the pan and shred with a fork, tossing with any juices. Set aside.

3. Lightly toast the chillies, then remove the stalks, seeds and veins. Break or cut up into small pieces, then place in saucepan with boiling water to cover. Simmer for 15–20 minutes or until they plump up.

4. In a blender or food processor, combine the chillies, garlic, oregano, cumin, stock and lime juice until it forms a smooth paste.

5. Heat the meat in its juices and pan drippings, then add the sauce and mix well. Simmer over a low heat for about 20 minutes or until the meat has absorbed the chilli sauce. Season with salt and pepper, and adjust the cumin and oregano to taste.

6. Warm the tortillas. Into each one, spoon a generous portion of meat, a ladle of beans, then a sprinkling of onion and salsa to taste. Roll up tightly and serve straight away, while still hot. Accompany with guacamole and extra salsa.

NUTRITIONAL INFORMATION				
	TOTAL FAT	SAT FAT	CHOL	ENERGY
Total	123g	39g	735mg	4293kcals/18106kJ
Per Serving	31g	10g	184mg	1073kcals/4526kJ

VARIATIONS
TIME SAVING

Use 3tbsp mild chilli powder mixed with 1tbsp paprika in place of the whole chillies.

CHIMICHANGAS

These are a speciality of the regions that straddle the U.S./Mexican border along Arizona. Though any burrito can be turned into a chimichanga, this meaty one is particularly nice. Prepare burritos, folding carefully so that all of the filling is well wrapped. Secure each with a cocktail stick. Fry burrito/ chimichangas in 2.5cm/1in hot oil until browned on both sides. Drain on absorbent kitchen paper and serve with salsa of choice, guacamole, soured cream and chopped spring onion or coriander.

LOWER FAT

Use a simmered meat mixture instead of the one in the above recipe. Shred and season with cumin and mild chilli powder. Brown with 1 chopped onion and several cloves of chopped garlic in a nonstick pan with a little oil. Instead of frying burrito/chimichangas, brush the outside of each parcel lightly with oil, then bake in the oven at 190–200°C/375–400°F/Gas Mark 5–6 long enough to heat through, about 15 minutes. Serve straight away, with fromage frais or goat's cheese crumbled over the top, shredded lettuce and diced tomatoes and salsa of choice.

CHAPTER TWO

STREET FOODS
AND MARISCOS

★ ★ ★ ★ ★

TORTAS

PLUMP SANDWICHES OF TOASTED ROLLS FILLED WITH VARIED MIXTURES

Walk down the streets of any Mexican town and you will see the signs for tortas, or sandwiches. Often the word is simply scrawled on the outside of a shop window, or the side of the shop front. Sometimes it is a wooden sign saying no more.
Filled with anything from mashed beans and sardines to chorizo and salad, and/or melted cheese and ham, they are crisp-crusted, hot and satisfying.

MOLLETES

TORTAS FILLED WITH REFRIED PINTO BEANS
AND TANGY CABBAGE SALAD

Molletes are crusty rolls stuffed with hot melted beans and cheese, then garnished with a tangy, hot condiment such as pickled jalapeños. These molletes are more deluxe however: the beans are enriched with browned bacon and/or spicy chorizo, tomatoes and spices, then topped with crunchy cabbage salad.

SERVES 4

4 rolls, cut in halves and slightly hollowed out	½tsp ground cumin or to taste
vegetable oil or bacon fat	½ cabbage, thinly sliced
1 onion, chopped	about 2tbsp sliced pickled jalapeños, plus a little of the pickling liquid
3 cloves garlic, chopped	1tbsp olive oil
3 rashers bacon, chopped, or 2 chorizos, cut up	3tbsp white wine or cider vinegar
8 ripe tomatoes (450g/1lb), peeled and chopped	salt and pepper
1 recipe Refried Beans (page 76), or use canned, warmed with a little water	crumbled oregano to taste
	275g/10oz white cheese, grated

1. Preheat the oven to 200°C/400°F/Gas Mark 6. Brush the hollowed out rolls with oil or bacon fat. Toast in the oven until crisp and lightly golden brown.

2. Meanwhile, sauté the onion, garlic and bacon or chorizo until the onion is softened. Add the tomatoes and cook until saucy.

3. Add the beans and stir through so that they combine with the onion, tomatoes, etc. Season with cumin and set aside; keep warm.

4. Combine the cabbage with the jalapeños, olive oil and vinegar. Season with salt, pepper and crumbled oregano.

5. Fill the rolls with the warm bean mixture then top with the cheese. Close up and warm through in oven. Open and fill with the cabbage salad. Serve immediately.

NUTRITIONAL INFORMATION				
	TOTAL FAT	SAT FAT	CHOL	ENERGY
Total	164g	63g	277mg	2956kcals/12390kJ
Per Serving	41g	16g	69mg	739kcals/3097kJ

VARIATION
TIME SAVING

Simply warm already prepared refried beans (homemade or canned); season with chilli powder and cumin. Pile into lightly toasted hollowed out rolls, top with cheese and melt. Serve with pickled jalapeños, chopped onions soured cream.

TORTAS DE SARDINAS Y CHORIZO

ROLLS STUFFED WITH SARDINES AND CHORIZO

Crusty rolls are hollowed out and filled with a mixture of mashed sardines, browned chorizo, crisp raw onion and tangy pickled jalapeños. What makes these different is that they are left overnight for the juices to soak into the bread. Just before serving, toast until crisp and lightly golden brown. Bite into it for a delicious contrast of tastes and textures.

Sardines, by the way, are often mashed and combined with chorizo for all sorts of snacks and fillings: tostadas and tacos in addition to tortas.

SERVES 4

2 chorizo sausages, about 350g/12oz in total, skinned and broken up

½ can sardines, mashed with a fork

½tsp oregano, crumbled, or more to taste

4–6tbsp sliced pickled jalapeños or more, to taste, plus a little of the pickling liquid

4 medium rolls or 8 small rolls, cut in halves and slightly hollowed out

little olive oil for brushing onto the rolls

1. Brown the chorizo until it cooks into a savoury mashed mixture. Remove from the heat and leave to cool.

2. Mix with the onion, sardines, oregano and jalapeños plus a little of the liquid.

3. Stuff the mixture into the rolls, then close and squeeze tightly. Place the rolls into a plastic bag and refrigerate overnight to let the juices soak into the bread.

4. Preheat the oven to 220°C/425°F/Gas Mark 7. Brush the outside of the rolls with oil. Bake in the oven or brown in a heavy pan, tossing and turning occasionally, until the rolls are golden brown on the outside and heated through inside.

5. Serve hot, straight away, with extra jalapeños en escabeche if liked.

NUTRITIONAL INFORMATION				
	TOTAL FAT	SAT FAT	CHOL	ENERGY
Total	102g	40g	216mg	1720kcals/7192kJ
Per Serving	25g	10g	54mg	430kcals/1798kJ

TORTA DEL MERCADO
MARKETPLACE TORTAS

I ate this torta one day in a Michoacan marketplace; the meat itself was very savoury and deliciously flavoured. This is especially good with any highly flavoured not too lean leftover roast.

SERVES 4

about 350g/12oz cooked tender pork, diced	3tbsp chopped jicama, peeled and diced
2 onions, chopped	3 tomatoes, diced
3 garlic cloves, chopped	2–3 pickled jalapeño chillies, chopped
1tbsp oil	1tbsp chopped fresh coriander
salt and pepper	juice of ½ lime
mild chilli powder, such as New Mexico or guajillo, to taste	4 rolls
large pinch marjoram	about 3tbsp soured cream

1. Brown the meat and half the onion with the garlic in the oil. Season with salt, pepper, chilli powder and marjoram.
2. Combine the jicama, tomatoes, jalapeños, coriander and remaining onion with the lime juice. Season with salt and pepper.
3. Hollow out the rolls and lightly toast. Smear the insides with the soured cream.
4. Combine the hot meat with salsa and spoon into the rolls. Serve immediately.

NUTRITIONAL INFORMATION

	TOTAL FAT	SAT FAT	CHOL	ENERGY
Total	48g	18g	412mg	1398kcals/5882kJ
Per Serving	12g	4g	103mg	350kcals/1470kJ

VARIATION
LOWER FAT

Fromage frais can be used in place of the soured cream. Turkey thigh makes a good substitute for the pork, although much of the pork available these days is lean if trimmed well.

BASIC GARNACHAS

Garnachas, gorditas (little fat ones) and chalupas (boats) are all little cuplike containers based on masa harina, which are filled with various savoury fillings and crunchy salads, tostada-like.

They can be quite small and appetizer size; they might be served in a bar, at a makeshift stall on a street corner, or in a restaurant heaped onto a platter in a dazzling assortment, to be nibbled on greedily with drinks before the rest of the meal.

225g/8oz masa harina	225ml/8fl oz cold water
3tbsp olive oil	vegetable oil, as needed
½tsp salt	

1. Combine the masa harina with the olive oil and salt, and work in well.
2. Stir in the cold water, working the dough until it forms a smooth pliable but not too sticky dough.
3. Roll into eight balls for garnachas or gorditas, four balls for chalupas. Flatten each and using your fingers mould a little lip around each edge.
4. Fry in hot oil until golden, then drain on absorbent kitchen paper. To reheat, place on baking sheet in the oven at 190–200°C/375–400°F/Gas Mark 5–6 until crisp edged and warm through.

NUTRITIONAL INFORMATION

	TOTAL FAT	SAT FAT	CHOL	ENERGY
Total	36g	5g	0mg	1064kcals/4482kJ

VARIATION
LOWER FAT

I like this way of making garnachas better than the traditional, which can be very heavy. These are lighter; crisp on the outside, corn tasting and tender inside. Place the little masa shapes on an oiled baking sheet and bake in the oven at 200°C/400°F/Gas Mark 6 for about 15–20 minutes. The edges should brown a little and the little shapes should not fall apart when lifted off the sheet with a spatula. They will not, however, turn as golden as the fried ones do.

GARNACHAS GUADALAJARA

GARNACHAS WITH CHORIZO, POTATO, CARROT AND NOPALES

SERVES 4

1 large potato	pinch oregano
½ carrot, diced	pinch ground cinnamon
1tsp vinegar	pinch ground cumin
2 chorizo sausage, 350g/12oz, casing removed, skinned and cut into small pieces	1 recipe Basic Garnachas shapes (page 42)
1 onion, chopped	175ml/6fl oz soured cream
1 clove garlic, chopped	Pickled Onion Rings (page 71)
1 tomato, diced	1tbsp chopped fresh coriander
75g/3oz nopale cactus, cooked and drained (or green beans, cut into bite-sized pieces)	

1. Par-boil the potato until almost but not quite tender. Add the carrot towards the end of cooking and cook with the potato. Remove the carrot and leave to cool. Rinse the potato and cool. Peel, dice and sprinkle with vinegar, then set aside.

2. Brown the chorizo in a frying pan over medium heat. Add the onion, garlic and tomato when chorizo is half cooked through. Add the potato, carrot and nopale or green beans. Season with oregano, cinnamon, cumin and chipotle. Warm through together, then set aside and keep warm.

3. Heap each garnacha with several spoonfuls of filling, then top with a dollop of soured cream, a sprinkling of both pickled onions and coriander. Serve straight away, with extra chipotle or pickled jalapeños on the side.

NUTRITIONAL INFORMATION				
	TOTAL FAT	SAT FAT	CHOL	ENERGY
Total	192g	67g	245mg	3691kcals/15454kJ
Per Serving	48g	17g	61mg	923kcals/3864kJ

GARNACHAS OAXAQUENO

MASA CUPS FILLED WITH REFRIED BEANS, SAVOURY PORK
AND TANGY CABBAGE SALAD

These garnachas are filled with refried beans, carnitas and a tangy raw cabbage and carrot salad.

SERVES 4

¼ cabbage	8 Garnachas (page 42)
1tbsp olive oil	1 recipe Refried Beans (page 76), warmed
2tbsp lime juice	
2 cloves garlic, chopped	1 recipe Carnitas or other meat (page 79), chopped and browned in a pan, warmed
1 carrot, grated	
salt to taste	½ onion, chopped
pinch thyme	
hot pepper sauce from a bottle to taste	

1. Combine the cabbage with the olive oil, lime juice, garlic, carrot, salt, thyme and hot pepper sauce to taste.

2. Preheat the oven to 200°C/400°F/Gas Mark 6. Heat the garnachas on a baking sheet in the oven for about 5–8 minutes.

3. Fill the little masa shapes with warm refried beans, then top with browned meat, chopped onion and the cabbage salad. Serve straight away.

NUTRITIONAL INFORMATION				
	TOTAL FAT	SAT FAT	CHOL	ENERGY
Total	190g	39g	635mg	4635kcals/19497kJ
Per Serving	47.5g	10g	158mg	1159kcals/4874kJ

VARIATION
LOWER FAT

Omit the olive oil from the cabbage-carrot salad and take care that the meat you use is well drained of any fat.

SALBUTES NEGRITOS

YUCATECAN SNACKS OF MASA AND BEANS TOPPED WITH MEAT
AND CRUNCHY VEGETABLE SALAD

This snack of black bean-enriched tortillas, fried to a crisp and topped with a variety of savoury toppings, is the most often found snack in the Yucatan.

SERVES 4

225g/8oz masa harina	Pickled Onion Rings (page 71)
2tbsp plain flour	¼ cabbage, thinly sliced
½tsp salt	1–2 fairly mild green or yellow chillies, seeded and chopped
2–3tbsp black beans, puréed and thinned with a little of the cooking liquid	1–2 ripe tomatoes, chopped
4tbsp water or black bean cooking liquid	handful of toasted pumpkin seeds
oil for frying	pinch oregano, crushed
225–350g/8–12oz chilli-flavoured cooked pork, beef, or chicken (see any recipe for tacos, Tostadas on page 73)	

1. Mix the masa with the flour and salt, then add the beans and enough of the water or bean liquid to make a stiff dough. Leave to stand for 5–10 minutes.
2. Roll the mixture into 2.5cm/1in balls and flatten into 10cm/4in rounds. Cook each tortilla on a hot ungreased frying pan or comal, stacking them as they cook.
3. Heat the oil to a depth of about 2.5cm/1in, then fry each tortilla in hot oil until crisp. Drain on absorbent kitchen paper.
4. Top each hot crisp tortilla with meat or chicken, pickled onion, cabbage, chillies, tomatoes, pumpkin seeds and oregano. Eat immediately.

NUTRITIONAL INFORMATION	TOTAL FAT	SAT FAT	CHOL	ENERGY
Total	25g	5.75g	171mg	1611kcals/6807kJ
Per Serving	6g	1.5g	43mg	402kcals/1701kJ

CHALUPAS AL ASADOR

MASA BOATS FILLED WITH BARBECUED MEAT, BLACK BEANS AND CHORIZO

A good snack to remember when you have a solitary chop left from yesterday's barbecue. I have eaten this made with both pork and goat, but lamb or beef would be good, too.

SERVES 4

4tbsp soured cream	100–175g/4–6oz barbecued meat, cut up or shredded, heated through
grated rind of ¼ lime	1 avocado, peeled, stoned and sliced
juice of ½ lime	3–5 radishes, diced
1 chorizo or spicy blood sausage, such as morcilla	handful of watercress leaves, coarsely chopped
4 chalupa shapes or 8 Garnachas (page 42)	fresh salsa of choice
1 recipe Refried Black Beans (page 76), warmed	
about 75g/3oz white crumbly cheese, such as not too salty feta or fresh pecorino, crumbled	

1. Combine the soured cream with the lime rind and juice. Set aside.
2. Pan brown the sausage until crisp and browned; set aside and keep warm.
3. Preheat the oven to 200°C/400°F/Gas Mark 6. Heat the chalupa shapes on a baking sheet in the oven for about 15–20 minutes or until warm.
4. Fill each chalupa with warm beans, then sprinkle with cheese. Top with a little of the browned sausage, the barbecued meat, diced avocado, radishes, watercress and a spoonful of the lime-flavoured cream. Offer salsa of choice on the side.

NUTRITIONAL INFORMATION	TOTAL FAT	SAT FAT	CHOL	ENERGY
Total	234g	66g	245mg	4468kcals/18732kJ
Per Serving	58g	17g	61mg	1117kcals/4683kJ

NARANJA CON CHILE A LA YUCATECA
YUCATECAN ORANGES

Outside the ruins of Chichen Itza, on a day thick with jungle heat, I cooled myself with the following snack purchased from a makeshift stall. It is a classic nibble in the Yucatan, where the juicy citrus flavour combined with the hot pepper is cooling; the small amount of salt is surprisingly refreshing since it helps retain liquid that is so easily evaporating in the relentless heat.

SERVES 4

4 ripe oranges, peeled, seeded and sliced

cayenne pepper to taste

paprika to taste

sugar and salt as liked

1. Arrange the oranges on a plate, including their juices.

2. Sprinkle with cayenne, paprika, sugar and salt.

3. Leave to chill for 1 hour or so before serving.

NUTRITIONAL INFORMATION				
	TOTAL FAT	SAT FAT	CHOL	ENERGY
Total	0g	0g	0mg	237kcals/1011kJ
Per Serving	0g	0g	0mg	59kcals/253kJ

VARIATION
OTHER FRUITS

Ripe sweet mangos sliced and splashed with lime juice, or pineapple chunks, sliced melon or watermelon are all delicious prepared as for the above oranges.

TAMALES DE ELOTE
FRESH CORN TAMALES

Tamales are often sold from tamale vendors, fished out from big pots that are fragrant with the smell of steaming corn husks. Tamales may be filled with savoury ingredients or with sweet ones. During the season of the sweetest corn, they are made with fresh corn such as these.

SERVES 4

corn husks	100ml/4fl oz water or as needed
75g/3oz butter, softened	2 onions, toasted and diced
225g/8oz masa	salt and black pepper or mild chilli powder to taste
½tsp baking powder	pinch sugar, if needed
350g/12oz cooked sweetcorn kernels (canned is fine; use the liquid when required)	salsa of choice, preferably tangy lemon-limy salsa

1. Place the corn husks in a bowl and pour boiling water over them to cover. Cover the bowl and leave to soften for about 30 minutes.

2. Using a wooden spoon or food processor, combine the butter with the masa and baking powder.

3. Blend the sweetcorn in a blender or food processor until it forms a chunky purée, with half of the corn still in kernels, the rest a creamy mixture.

4. Work the corn purée into the masa-butter mixture, then continue adding water until it forms the consistency desired – moist but not too sticky, firm but not hard and crumbly.

5. Place two or three corn husks on a plate or in the palm of your hand. On top of this, place several spoonfuls of the filling, onions and season to taste. Fold over, first the sides, then the top and bottom, to fully enclose the filling.

6. Place each husk-wrapped parcel in the top of a steamer, then steam the parcels for 40 minutes or until they feel firm. After 30 minutes take one out to sample it. Top up the water as needed.

7. Serve the tamales either straight away, or reheat later or the next day. Accompany with salsa of choice.

NUTRITIONAL INFORMATION				
	TOTAL FAT	SAT FAT	CHOL	ENERGY
Total	69g	42g	173mg	1790kcals/7532kJ
Per Serving	17g	10g	43mg	448kcals/1883kJ

VARIATION
CHILLI CHEESE TAMALES

Fresh corn tamales are delicious with the addition of roasted mild green chilli and white cheese. Choose a roasted, peeled, seeded and sliced poblano or Anaheim chilli. Select a cheese such as Cheddar or combination of Cheddar and tangy mild white goat's cheese. Place a nugget of each inside the corn filling, then fold and wrap as above.

APPERATIVE DE JICAMA

JICAMA SNACK OR APPETIZER

WITH CHILLI

On a hot, sultry day there are few foods lighter and more refreshing than sliced jicama, sprinkled with salt, fiery cayenne chilli and a splash of lime juice. Jicama is a root whose white flesh looks very much like a potato and tastes somewhat like an apple.

Sold in the streets of many Mexican towns, they are often skewered with fruit, to be nibbled while you continue along your way, but they are equally good arranged on a platter and eaten sitting down.

Watermelon, pineapple, mango (either ripe or green), papaya and oranges are all delicious added to the fruit plate (I omit the salt when including the other, sweeter, fruits).

SERVES 4

½ medium jicama, peeled and cut into bite-sized pieces	cayenne pepper to taste
½ lime	salt to taste

1. Arrange the jicama on a plate and squeeze the lime over. Chill if liked.

2. When ready to serve, sprinkle with cayenne and salt to taste.

VARIATION
GREEN MANGO

Peel 1–2 green mangos and remove the stone. Cut into small bite-sized slices. Sprinkle with lime, cayenne and salt to taste. Leave to stand for at least 30 minutes, then eat as liked.

GARBANZOS CON CHILES

CHICKPEAS WITH SALSA, CORIANDER AND LIME

On every street and village throughout Mexico at various times of the day, vendors set up simple stalls and sell a variety of foods. In Guadalajara I often bought the following snack of tender boiled chickpeas, wrapped in a paper cone, splashed with salsa and lime. Spicy and hot they are irresistible for afternoon walking and munching. Amounts don't matter much – your own personal taste is all. Use the following as a guide only.

SERVES 4

450g/1lb cooked drained chickpeas (canned are fine)	3–5tbsp chopped fresh coriander
salt to taste	1 onion, finely chopped
hot salsa or bottled hot sauce as liked	wedges of lime

1. Season the chickpeas with salt to taste. Mix with the salsa or hot sauce, coriander and onion. Serve at room temperature, with wedges of lime to squeeze over.

NUTRITIONAL INFORMATION				
	TOTAL FAT	SAT FAT	CHOL	ENERGY
Total	13g	1g	0mg	545kcals/2308kJ
Per Serving	3g	0.3g	0mg	136kcals/577kJ

BEBIDAS
COOLING DRINKS

O̲n any sweltering day, by the time the sun has barely made its way up, stalls are already set up for refreshing fruit drinks. Blenders whirling away turn out creamy refreshments of milk, fruit, juices and drinks based on crushed rice.

LIQUADA DES FRUTAS
FRUIT MILKSHAKES
FROM THE STREETS OF MEXICO

I̲n every street, marketplace and bus station you will find counters piled high with fragrant sweet fruit. Again blenders whirling away, stopping every so often to pour out big glasses of sweet fruit drinks. Sometimes a little yogurt is added; at other times no milk at all, simply tropical fruits and their juices. Though strawberries sound rather pedestrian, they are worth noting for their exquisite refreshment, and because I will never forget the sweet pink glassfuls that got me through my first hot and sweaty visit to Mexico's capital city.

SERVES 2

225g/8oz strawberries
2tbsp icing sugar
225ml/8fl oz milk
few drops vanilla essence
crushed ice

1. Whirl all the ingredients together in a blender until frothy. Drink straight away.

NUTRITIONAL INFORMATION

	TOTAL FAT	SAT FAT	CHOL	ENERGY
Total	0.5g	0.25g	2mg	229kcals/974kJ
Per Serving	0.25g	0.1g	1mg	114kcals/487kJ

VARIATIONS

Other fruits to choose when making milkshakes: cantaloupe, apricots, bananas, peach. Try mango using yogurt instead of milk. And do try papaya, pineapple and/or watermelon using water or white grape juice instead of milk.

HORCHATA CON FRUTAS

SWEET RICE-MILK
WITH TROPICAL FRUIT AND NUTS

Horchata is made by soaking uncooked rice in flavoured water until it softens, then puréeing it with sugar and flavourings. It makes a nourishing, comforting and refreshing drink with a "milky" consistency but completely non-dairy.

SERVES 4

225g/8oz rice

1 litre/1¾pt water

1 10-cm/1¼-in cinnamon stick, broken into several pieces

3tbsp pecans

¼–½tsp vanilla essence

75g/3oz sugar or to taste

2 cactus fruits, peeled and sieved to deseed (or mango, peeled, stoned and diced)

½–1 sweet ripe melon, such as cantaloupe or Galia, peeled, seeded and diced

juice of ½ lime

1. Combine the rice, water and cinnamon stick and leave overnight at room temperature or in the refrigerator.

2. When the rice is softened the next day, remove the cinnamon stick.

3. Place the rice in the blender with the pecans, vanilla essence and sugar. Purée until quite smooth.

4. Add the cactus fruit, melon and lime juice, and repeat whirling in the blender.

5. Serve straight away, strained through a sieve, and poured over ice cubes. Since the rice settles and the drink separates quite quickly, horchata should be freshly blended just before serving. (May be prepared ahead of time, up until the adding of the fruit. Blend with the fruit just before serving.)

NUTRITIONAL INFORMATION				
	TOTAL FAT	SAT FAT	CHOL	ENERGY
Total	34g	2.5g	0mg	1521kcals/6435kJ
Per Serving	8.5g	0.5g	0mg	380kcals/1609kJ

VARIATION
TIME SAVING

Use rice powder instead of steeping whole rice overnight. Combine rice powder with milk, sugar or honey to taste, vanilla and cinnamon. Blend with crushed ice until frothy, then serve straight away.

MARISCOS

THE SEAFOOD STALL

From seaside villages to cities such as the capital Mexico City, tiny shacks and
restaurants dot the streets serving fresh, briny seafood.

COCKTEL DE MARISCOS

SEAFOOD COCKTAIL
WITH CHILLIES, ORANGE AND SPRING ONION

Any seafood could be used here: plump prawns or langoustine, rings of chewy squid, mussels plucked from their shells.

The fiery citrus salsa is typical of salsas from the Southeastern coast of Mexico, from Vera Cruz south through the Yucatan. A drop or two is probably all you will need; save leftovers for brightening up nearly anything else – soups and stews, tacos, seafood, grilled foods, rice and beans. If your chillies are not blisteringly hot, you might want to increase the amount so that the sauce packs a good punch; if your chillies are terribly hot, decrease amounts to about half that called for (it should be spicy, not painful).

SERVES 4

4–6 spring onions, thinly sliced

½ red habanero chilli, roasted, charred, peeled, seeded and coarsely chopped

½–1 fresh red chilli, such as jalapeño, roasted, charred, peeled, seeded and coarsely chopped

100ml/4fl oz orange juice,

plus a little pulp

75ml/3fl oz lime juice, preferably freshly squeezed

salt to taste

450g/1lb prawns in their shells

round or Cos lettuce leaves

1 lime, cut into wedges

1 orange, cut into wedges

1. Combine the spring onions with habanero and jalapeño chillies, then stir in the orange juice, lime juice and salt. Leave to stand for at least 10 minutes, preferably up to 3 hours.

2. Cook the prawns over high heat until bubbles form around the edge, remove from the heat, and leave to cool. Then drain, peel and slit down the backs, removing the veins. Serve the cooked seafood on leaves of crisp lettuce and sprinkle a few drops of the sauce onto them. Serve with lime and orange wedges and additional hot sauce.

NUTRITIONAL INFORMATION				
	TOTAL FAT	SAT FAT	CHOL	ENERGY
Total	4g	1g	473mg	333kcals/1413kJ
Per Serving	1g	0.25g	118mg	83kcals/353kJ

VARIATION

Instead of prawns, try 450g/1lb squid, cleaned and cut into rings and tentacles, 1kg/2lb clams or mussels, or any other fresh seafood or combination that is available.

CEVICHE

MARINATED AND CITRUS-PICKLED FISH APPETIZER

SERVES 4

450g/1lb fish fillets (haddock, sole, snapper, sierra or similar), skinned and bones removed

175ml/6fl oz freshly squeezed lemon juice (juice of 3 lemons)

175ml/6fl oz freshly squeezed lime juice (juice of 3 limes)

2tsp oregano leaves, crushed

½tsp cumin seeds, lightly toasted and left whole

2 ripe tomatoes, finely diced

1 small to medium red onion, chopped

1–2 green serrano chillies, chopped or as liked

4tbsp chopped fresh coriander

2tbsp chopped fresh mint

1 stick celery, chopped or thinly sliced

10–15 pimento-stuffed green olives, sliced

2tbsp sliced jalapeños en escabeche (pickled jalapeño chillies) or as liked

100ml/4fl oz freshly squeezed orange juice

1tsp salt or to taste

2tbsp olive oil

1. Cut the fish into 1cm/½in cubes. Place in a glass container with the lemon juice, lime juice and oregano. Mix well, then cover and leave in the refrigerator overnight. Do not leave for longer than 12 hours or the fish will go mushy.

2. Drain the fish and add the toasted cumin seeds, tomatoes, onion, chilli, coriander, mint, celery, green olives, jalapeños en escabeche, orange juice, salt and olive oil.

3. Chill before serving. This dish can be refrigerated for up to 3 days.

NUTRITIONAL INFORMATION				
	TOTAL FAT	SAT FAT	CHOL	ENERGY
Total	29g	4g	162mg	714kcals/3003kJ
Per Serving	7g	1g	41mg	178kcals/751kJ

FIAMBRE DE JAIBA

SPICY CRAB SALAD

In the Yucatan, where temperatures soar to almost unbearable heights, you will find salady dishes called fiambre – cool mixtures of hot and spicy ingredients. Their flash of hot chilli and cool crisp texture refresh and stimulate appetites grown sluggish from the assault of the day's heat. Often these fiambres are rolled up in tender fresh tortillas for hot-weather tacos.

SERVES 4

3 shallots or ¼ red onion, finely chopped

1 fresh chilli, such as jalapeño or serrano, chopped

juice of ½ lime

1tbsp white wine or fruit vinegar

1tsp fresh marjoram or ½tsp chopped fresh oregano

1tsp chopped fresh coriander

1tbsp olive oil

225–350g/8–12oz fresh crab meat

1 avocado, peeled and sliced

radishes, thinly sliced

1. Combine the shallots or onion with the chilli, lime juice, vinegar, marjoram, coriander and olive oil. Mix lightly with the crab.

2. Serve garnished with the avocado and radishes.

NUTRITIONAL INFORMATION

	TOTAL FAT	SAT FAT	CHOL	ENERGY
Total	52g	9g	162mg	682kcals/2826kJ
Per Serving	13g	2g	41mg	170kcals/707kJ

VARIATION

Chillies Rellenos con Fiambre: Omit the chilli from the filling mixture. Prepare large green chillies, such as poblano or Anaheim, by roasting, peeling and removing the inner core and seeds. Fill with the above crab mixture and serve chilled, on a bed of lettuce, garnished with avocado and radishes.

CHAPTER THREE

THE HOME KITCHEN

★ ★ ★ ★ ★

THE HOME KITCHEN

DIPS, NACHOS, MELTED CHEESE DISHES, CUP TAMALES, SOUPS

The best Mexican food is rarely found in restaurants, even in Mexico. It is a unique blend of Central American, of Spanish, and of the Arab cooking which in its turn influenced Spain. It can be brutally simple, or extremely complex: indeed, the same dish may well be prepared in ways which reflect the various influences in very varying degrees, so you may have an Aztec version, a poor Spanish soldiers' version, a rich hidalgo's version, and a Moorish version. Here are several recipes that are found throughout Mexico, in almost every home – everyday, staple, simple dishes.

TOTOPOS O NACHOS CON ELOTES Y FRIJOLES

BLACK BEAN AND CORN NACHOS

Nachos are simply toasted tortilla chips, topped with cheese and salsa and melted in the oven. From this basic beginning, nachos have come to encompass many delicious appetizers based on crisp tortilla chips.

SERVES 4-6

1 onion, chopped

3 cloves garlic, chopped

2tbsp olive oil

2tsp mild chilli powder, such as ancho, or pasilla or mixture that includes chipotle powder

450–700g/1–1½lb cooked black beans, plus about 100ml/4fl oz of their cooking liquid

salt and hot sauce to taste

1tsp cumin seeds

275g/10oz Cheddar cheese, thinly sliced

about 225g/8oz sweetcorn kernels, drained and warmed

3tbsp chopped fresh coriander

10 cherry tomatoes, quartered, or 2 ripe medium tomatoes, diced

1–2tbsp pickled jalapeños

tortilla chips, preferably low salt

1. Preheat the oven to 230°C/450°F/Gas Mark 8. Sauté the onion and garlic in the olive oil until softened, then sprinkle with chilli powder and cook a moment or two longer.

2. Add the black beans and their liquid, then cook down until it forms a thick paste. Mash the beans slightly as they cook. Season with salt and hot sauce to taste.

3. Spoon the bean mixture into a baking dish, then sprinkle with cumin seeds and cheese.

4. Bake until the cheese melts, then remove from the oven and spoon the warm corn around the edges. Sprinkle with the coriander and garnish with the tomatoes and pickled jalapeños. Serve straight away, accompanied by tortilla chips arranged around the edge in a sunflower-like pattern.

NUTRITIONAL INFORMATION				
	TOTAL FAT	SAT FAT	CHOL	ENERGY
Total	146g	68g	275mg	2644kcals/11069kJ
Per Serving (4)	36g	17g	69mg	661kcals/2767kJ
Per Serving (6)	24g	11g	46mg	441kcals/1845kJ

GUACAMOLE

The word Guacamole comes from the Nahuatl molli, meaning sauce, and aguacate, meaning avocado. This classic sauce can be varied at will: more onion or less, salsa for seasoning instead of the individual ingredients, a few pureed tomatillos instead of tomatoes.

Spoon it into chicken soup for sopa de aguacate; roll into warm corn tortillas for a quintessential family snack or picnic treat; spread over crisp tortillas it makes a sauce for tostadas compuestas.

Guacamole is eaten as a sauce for carne asado, spit-roasted chicken or even hamburgers (hamburguesas); and is there a more enticing snack than a bowl of freshly made guacamole surrounded by crisp tortilla chips?

Choosing the avocados is the most important part of the recipe. They should be black or dark-skinned, and firm to the touch with a slight give at the pointed top that indicates a softening flesh. If they are too soft and squishy, they may taste off. Even if you have somewhat past-it avocados, you can usually pare off the browned bits once the fruit is peeled. When avocados are too hard at the time of purchase they may never ripen, so they should always be at least slightly yielding when purchased.

To open, cut into halves and remove the stone. Scoop out the flesh with a spoon.

SERVES 4 - 6

3 ripe black avocados	salt and mild chilli pepper to taste
juice of 1–1½ lemons or limes	cayenne or Tabasco if needed
1 clove garlic, chopped	about ¼ hot green chilli, chopped
½ small to medium onion, chopped	¼tsp ground cumin (optional)
2–3 small to medium tomatoes, diced or chopped	1tbsp chopped fresh coriander

1. Coarsely mash the avocado with the lemon or lime juices. Mix with the garlic, onion, tomatoes, salt, mild chilli, cayenne or Tabasco if using, green chilli, cumin and coriander.

2. Mix lightly but well and season to taste.

NUTRITIONAL INFORMATION

	TOTAL FAT	SAT FAT	CHOL	ENERGY
Total	96g	23g	0mg	971kcals/4010kJ
Per Serving (4)	24g	6g	0mg	243kcals/1003kJ
Per Serving (6)	16g	4g	0mg	162kcals/668kJ

QUESO OAXAQUENO AL FORNO

BAKED WHITE CHEESE
WITH GREEN SALSA

In Oaxaca this dish would be prepared with queso Oaxaca, a milky fresh cheese somewhere between fresh mozzarella and fresh pecorino. Don't let the simplicity of the recipe fool you into thinking it is ordinary: the taste of fresh milky cheese with sharp green salsa, all warmed together, is memorable.

SERVES 4

2 balls of fresh mozzarella or other milky, slightly but not too salty, fresh cheese, sliced	about 225g/8oz Salsa Verde (page 68), or to taste
225g/8oz cooked tomatillos, puréed or chopped	8 corn tortillas, warmed

1. Preheat the oven to 200°C/400°F/Gas Mark 6. Arrange the cheese in a large baking dish or in individual ramekins.

2. Combine the tomatillos and salsa verde, then pour over cheese.

3. Bake for about 10 minutes or until the cheese melts softly and bubbles around the edges.

4. Serve straight away, accompanied by warm corn tortillas for dipping or for making tacos.

NUTRITIONAL INFORMATION

	TOTAL FAT	SAT FAT	CHOL	ENERGY
Total	40g	22g	111mg	1575kcals/6658kJ
Per Serving	10g	5.5g	28mg	394kcals/1665kJ

SNACK SOUPS

Though you are apt to find them in cafés and sold from street vendors, soup is a fixture of the Mexican home kitchen. No stove, it seems, is without a simmering pot full at any given time. Soups make comforting midnight snacks after a night of too much tequila, or a nourishing bowlful on a cool evening to follow a sultry day.

CALDO RANCHERA

RICH SPICY BROTH

WITH PUMPKIN OR PARSNIP, CHICKPEAS, MACARONI, CABBAGE AND CHEESE

This is a homely soup I have had spooned up in a little café one mild evening somewhere in the labyrinth-like streets of Mexico City.

SERVES 4–6

1 litre/1¾pt chicken or other flavourful stock

225ml/8fl oz water

about 175g/6oz parsnip or pumpkin, cut into bite-sized pieces (peeled if pumpkin)

1 onion, chopped

3 cloves garlic, chopped

2 tomatoes, diced

2 bay leaves

4tbsp chopped fresh coriander

225g/8oz macaroni, cooked and drained

225g/8oz cooked drained chickpeas

½ fresh red chilli, such as jalapeño, thinly sliced

¼ cabbage, thinly sliced

100–175g/4–6oz mild white cheese, grated

½ pickled jalapeño chilli, chopped, or to taste (or a little chipotle)

1 lime, cut into wedges

1. Combine the stock with the water, parsnip or pumpkin, onion, garlic, tomatoes, bay leaves and half the coriander. Bring to the boil then reduce the heat and simmer until the vegetables are quite tender. Taste for seasoning.

2. Add the macaroni, chickpeas, fresh red chilli and cabbage, and cook only a moment or two, to warm through.

3. Ladle into bowls and garnish each with a little jalapeño , a sprinkle of the remaining coriander and a wedge of lime.

NUTRITIONAL INFORMATION				
	TOTAL FAT	SAT FAT	CHOL	ENERGY
Total	45g	23g	100mg	1101kcals/4623kJ
Per Serving (4)	11g	6g	25mg	275kcals/1156kJ
Per Serving (6)	7.5g	4g	17mg	183kcals/770kJ

CALDO TLAPENO

CHICKEN SOUP

WITH AVOCADO, CHICKPEAS AND CHIPOTLES

Caldo Tlapeno – that bowl of rich clear chicken soup awash with small pieces of chicken and vegetables, studded with chickpeas and spiked with smoky hot chipotle chillies, has gone from being ladled out by street vendors to becoming a classic in the Mexican kitchen.

The soup is said to have originated in the Mexico City suburb of Tlapan, where on Sundays, the park came alive with families spending the day in the open air amid the greenery. The food vendors, each trying to capture the appetite of the strolling diners, concocted and added various ingredients to their dishes, in the hopes of selling their wares. One soup-seller hit upon the simple combination we think of today as Tlapan: avocado, chipotle, chickpeas, chicken stock and lime.

SERVES 4–6

3 cloves garlic, coarsely chopped

1 tbsp olive oil

2 courgettes, cut into bite-sized pieces

½ carrot, thinly sliced

1 litre/1¾pt chicken stock

350g/12oz cooked drained chickpeas

1–2 chipotle chillies en adobo, cut into strips, plus a little of the marinade

2 spring onions, thinly sliced

100–175g/4–6oz shredded chicken

1 avocado, peeled, stoned and diced

1 tbsp chopped fresh coriander

handful of tortilla chips, preferably low salt ones

1 lime, cut into wedges

1. Warm the garlic in the olive oil without browning. Add the courgettes, carrot, chicken stock and chickpeas, then bring to the boil. Reduce the heat and simmer for about 10 minutes or until vegetables are tender.

2. Ladle the soup into bowls and garnish each with a little chipotle, spring onions, shredded chicken, avocado, coriander, tortilla chips and wedges of lime.

NUTRITIONAL INFORMATION				
	TOTAL FAT	SAT FAT	CHOL	ENERGY
Total	78g	14g	76mg	1450kcals/6072kJ
Per Serving (4)	20g	3.5g	19mg	363kcals/1518kJ
Per Serving (6)	13g	2.5g	13mg	242kcals/1012kJ

VARIATION
POSOLE TLAPENO

Simmer cooked drained hominy in place of the chickpeas and garnish as above. The earthy, bland hominy is sensational with the smoky hot chipotle, creamy avocado and sharp tangy lime.

GAZPACHO CON NOPALES
SPICY GAZPACHO
WITH CACTUS

Gazpacho is thirst-quenching and cooling in any hot, parched climate. It becomes exotic and spicy in Mexico where the sharpness of lime, the dusting of earthy cumin, tropical vegetables such as tomatillos and cactus, pungent herbs such as coriander, flavour this invigorating bowlful. For extra crunch, use jicama in place of cucumber.

I like to keep a large jug full in my refrigerator – it can get one through the cruellest of heatwaves. On particularly languid nights, a drop of tequila or even vodka added enhances its refreshment.

SERVES 4-6

- 3 cloves garlic, chopped
- 450ml/16fl oz tomato juice
- 450ml/16fl oz stock, such as vegetable or beef
- 2 medium or 1 large cucumber, diced
- 1–2 ripe tomatoes, diced
- 175–225g/6–8oz cooked tomatillos, skins removed and lightly cut up or crushed
- 1 cactus pod, cooked and drained and cut into bite-sized pieces (or use canned, drained)
- 50ml/2fl oz olive oil
- 2tbsp red or white wine vinegar or lime juice
- 1tbsp cumin
- salt, pepper, thyme and hot sauce to taste
- about 8 small ice cubes

1. Combine all the ingredients and stir together to combine well. Chill for at least 2 hours.

2. Adjust the seasoning of salt, hot pepper and vinegar; cold foods usually need quite a bit of salt and hot pepper.

3. Serve each portion of gazpacho with 1 or 2 small ice cubes.

NUTRITIONAL INFORMATION

	TOTAL FAT	SAT FAT	CHOL	ENERGY
Total	51g	7g	0mg	639kcals/2652kJ
Per Serving (4)	13g	2g	0mg	160kcals/663kJ
Per Serving (6)	9g	1g	0mg	107kcals/442kJ

HUEVOS RANCHEROS

EGGS ON TORTILLAS

WITH WITH TOMATO-PEPPER SAUCE

Huevos rancheros is ubiquitous in Mexico; it can be served as a midnight feast or a late morning meal to start the day, or whenever. The dish is often served differently but it is always the same: tender eggs on a tortilla, blanketed in tomato-chilli sauce. Garnishes may vary: browned chorizo, grilled plantains or bananas, a covering of melted cheese, slices of avocado, a puddle of warm refried beans, a flurry of sliced fiery chillies on top of the salsa, a sprinkling of coriander. Sautéed mild green poblano chillies (rajas) make an excellent accompaniment. No matter how varied the dish might be, it always tastes utterly delicious: the eggs free-range and fresh, the sauce alive with fire and flavour.

SERVES 4

4 tortillas, warmed (page 74)

8 poached or gently fried eggs with runny yolks

450ml/16fl oz warmed Cooked Tomato Sauce, (page 77)

1tbsp chopped fresh coriander

1 or 2 fresh green chillies, such as jalapeño or serrano, thinly sliced

1. Place a tortilla on each plate.

2. Top each tortilla with 2 cooked eggs.

3. Spoon over the warm tomato-chilli sauce, then sprinkle with coriander and chilli. Serve straight away.

NUTRITIONAL INFORMATION

	TOTAL FAT	SAT FAT	CHOL	ENERGY
Total	70g	20g	1585mg	1513kcals/6359kJ
Per Serving	17.5g	5g	396mg	378kcals/1590kJ

HUEVOS MICHOACAN

Garnish with a little chopped chipotles, their adobo marinade or salsa, and diced browned bananas or plantains.

HUEVOS DEL CAMPESINA

Serve the egg-topped tortillas with a chunky rather than puréed sauce: sauté 2 onions with garlic and diced green pepper, then sprinkle with 1tsp ground cumin and ¼tsp cinnamon. Cook for a moment or two, then add 1kg/2lb diced tomatoes (either raw or first toasted and charred, then peeled before dicing). Simmer until saucelike and chunky. Season with salt and sugar to balance the acid-sweetness, then serve over the eggs. Garnish with chopped fresh coriander.

SOPA DE LIMA

YUCATECAN LIME SOUP
WITH TOASTED GARLIC AND CITRUS JUICES

Traditionally, this tangy soup is served with shredded chicken and chicken giblets added to the bowl. I like the lighter version below, with the meat and giblets saved for another dish: tacos, tortas or enchiladas.

SERVES 4–6

- 3 medium onions, finely chopped
- 2–3 limes, peeled, seeded and diced
- 2–3 serrano chillies, finely chopped
- ½ green pepper, chopped
- 1–1½tbsp olive oil
- 3–4 ripe tomatoes, diced (fresh is best)
- pinch oregano, crushed
- salt and pepper
- 10–15 cloves whole garlic, toasted in their skins, then peeled
- 1 litre/1¾pt chicken stock
- juice of ½ grapefruit, plus a little grated rind
- juice of ½ orange, plus a little grated rind
- 2tbsp finely chopped fresh coriander
- handful of tortilla chips, preferably low salt ones

1. Combine 1 chopped onion with the diced lime flesh and chopped chillies. Set aside.

2. Sauté the remaining onions with the green pepper in the olive oil until softened. Add the tomatoes, oregano, salt and pepper, toasted peeled garlic and chicken stock.

3. Bring to the boil, then reduce the heat and simmer for about 10 minutes or until the tomatoes are just cooked through and the soup is richly flavoured.

4. Just before serving, add the grapefruit and orange juice and rind and the coriander.

5. Place several tablespoons of the onion-chilli-lime mixture into each bowl, then ladle in the hot soup. Serve each bowlful garnished with tortilla chips.

NUTRITIONAL INFORMATION				
	TOTAL FAT	SAT FAT	CHOL	ENERGY
Total	36g	6g	0mg	806kcals/3383kJ
Per Serving (4)	9g	1.5g	0mg	202kcals/846kJ
Per Serving (6)	6g	1g	0mg	134kcals/564kJ

CHAPTER FOUR

THE SALSA BAR

★ ★ ★ ★ ★

THE SALSA BAR

Salsa literally means "sauce", but in the absence of other qualifications it normally means salsa cruda, "raw sauce", which appears on the table as regularly as pepper and salt. It is frequently used as a dip, with corn chips, but it can be spooned on to almost any savoury dish: omelettes, chiles rellenos, meat . . . you name it. There are also cooked salsas and, whether raw or cooked, most salsas crudas improve and mature (grow hotter!) if left overnight in the refrigerator. The basic ingredients, mixed-and-matched in a wide variety of combinations, are dried or fresh peppers; onions; tomatoes (including tomatillos); garlic, and cilantro (coriander). Optional additions include oregano, vinegar and olive oil.

SALSA CRUDA

BASIC MEXICAN SALSA OF UNCOOKED INGREDIENTS

This raw salsa is classic: for best flavour and fragrance, as well as maximum heat, make it freshly before serving. You can use fresh unpeeled tomatoes during high season; in the middle of winter, use canned. As for peeling – it is up to you.

2–3 cloves garlic, chopped

1 small to medium onion, chopped

1–2 fresh green chillies, such as jalapeño or serrano, or as desired, chopped

5–8 ripe tomatoes, diced or chopped

3tbsp chopped fresh coriander

salt to taste, sugar if needed to balance the acid of the tomatoes

cumin to taste (optional)

1. Combine all the salsa ingredients together.

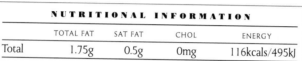

NUTRITIONAL INFORMATION			
	TOTAL FAT	SAT FAT	CHOL	ENERGY
Total	1.75g	0.5g	0mg	116kcals/495kJ

TROPICAL FRUIT SALSA

A selection of tropical fruit, diced and tossed with a little chilli and a squeeze of lime juice, makes a refreshing salsa that is especially good with grilled seafood or meat tacos.

¼ ripe sweet pineapple, peeled and diced

½ mango or papaya, peeled, seeded and diced

1 slice crisp watermelon, seeded and diced, or ¼ apple, seeded and diced, or 1 banana, peeled and diced

½–1 green chilli, such as jalapeño or serrano, chopped

½–1 red chilli, such as jalapeño or serrano, chopped

¼ red onion, chopped

1tbsp sugar

salt to taste

juice of ¼ lime

1. Combine all the salsa ingredients together and taste for seasoning. Serve straight away.

NUTRITIONAL INFORMATION			
	TOTAL FAT	SAT FAT	CHOL	ENERGY
Total	0.75g	0.1g	0mg	189kcals/802kJ

THE SALSA BAR

SALSA COCIDO DE JITOMATE Y CHILE FRESCO

COOKED TOMATO AND FRESH CHILLI SALSA

2–3 fresh green chillies, such as guero or Anaheim or poblano

6–8 medium tomatoes (use fresh, not canned for this recipe)

2–3 cloves garlic, chopped

salt to taste

juice of ½ lemon or lime

oregano to taste

1. Place the chillies in a saucepan with water to cover. Boil covered, for 5–10 minutes or until the chillies are tender. Remove from the liquid and leave until cool enough to handle.
2. While the chillies are cooling, place the tomatoes in saucepan with water to just cover and bring to the boil. Cook over a high heat for about 5–8 minutes or until the tomatoes are tender and liquid partly evaporated. Remove the tomato skins out of the mixture and discard.
3. Cut the stalks off the chillies and remove the skin and seeds. Coarsely chop the flesh.
4. Using a pestle and mortar or blender, purée the garlic with salt. Work in the chilli flesh, then the tomato flesh, adding just enough of the tomato cooking liquid to form a smoothish sauce.
5. Season with lemon juice and oregano to taste, and more salt if needed.

NUTRITIONAL INFORMATION			
	TOTAL FAT	SAT FAT	CHOL	ENERGY
Total	2g	0.5g	0mg	112kcals/481kJ

SALSA VERDE DE TOMATILLO

GREEN SALSA OF CHILLIES AND TOMATILLOS

Husk tomatoes, astringent and sour, are at their best cooked into a tart purée and used as a basis for the green sauces, or salsas, that form refreshing contrast to the richer dishes. This makes a delicious salsa of cooked tomatillas combined with raw onion, garlic and coriander; for a sauce to use for cooking, the aromatics will be stewed with the tomatillas. This salsa has just a little bite – for a more aggressive character add more (or hotter) chillies. For a milder sauce, use only one chilli combined with one chopped sweet green pepper. Use the mild sauce to cook with: simmer with chicken or pork for classic green chilli dishes.

450g/1lb tomatillos, quartered, or 450g/1lb can tomatillos

1–2 fresh hot chillies, such as jalapeños, chopped

1 small onion, chopped

2 cloves garlic, chopped

1tbsp chopped fresh coriander

salt and cumin to taste

1. If using raw tomatillos, quarter and place them in a saucepan with water to cover. Bring to the boil, then reduce the heat and simmer until soft but not too mushy, about 10 minutes. Drain gently, saving some of the liquid in case you need it for the salsa. If using canned tomatillos, do not cook, just open the can and gently drain.
2. Place the cooked or canned tomatillos in a blender or processor with the chillies, onion, garlic and coriander. Blend until the mixture reaches the consistency desired: it may be preferred smoother or chunkier. Add a little of the cooking liquid if needed, for consistency.
3. Season to taste with salt and cumin.

NUTRITIONAL INFORMATION			
	TOTAL FAT	SAT FAT	CHOL	ENERGY
Total	0.5g	neg	0mg	102kcals/434kJ

X-NIPEK
"DOG SNOUT" SALSA

This Yucatecan salsa is fiery hot. It is said to be called Dog Snout because its pungent fumes make one's nose run uncontrollably, like the wet nose of a dog!

2 habanero or Scots bonnet chillies, or more if preferred	juice of ½ lime
2 cloves garlic, toasted	⅛tsp oregano, crushed
1tsp salt	2–3 spring onions, thinly sliced
juice of ½ orange, plus grated rind of ¼ orange	1tbsp chopped fresh coriander

1. Purée the chillies with the garlic, salt, orange juice, orange rind and lime juice.
2. Season with oregano, then stir in the spring onions and coriander.

NUTRITIONAL INFORMATION			
	TOTAL FAT	SAT FAT	CHOL	ENERGY
Total	0.2g	neg	0mg	22kcals/93kJ

SALSA DE CHILES PICANTE
HOT DRIED RED CHILLI SAUCE

Make a double or triple quantity of this powerful sauce; it keeps at least a month and is handy to shake onto anything that needs a bit of fire.

5 or smallish dried hot red chillies (such as cayenne or Arbol; don't use bird's eye as they are too hot)	100ml/4fl oz white wine vinegar
	½tsp salt

1. Crumble the chillies into small pieces. Purée the chillies with the vinegar and salt.

NUTRITIONAL INFORMATION			
	TOTAL FAT	SAT FAT	CHOL	ENERGY
Total	0g	0g	0mg	29kcals/116kJ

SALSA DE CHILES AL CARBON
SCORCHED CHILLI SALSA

Lightly scorching the chillies imparts a slightly smoky taste, and makes the little peppers easy to peel. *Take care of your fingers, as the heat can linger and linger, lying in wait for you to innocently wipe your eyes and plunging you into pain.* The green pepper in this salsa add a pepper flavour without the heat of all the chillies. If you prefer it hotter, use 2 Anaheim or poblanos, or 3 jalapeños in place of the green pepper.

1 green pepper	juice of ½ lime or to taste
1 large mild chilli, such as Anaheim or poblano	1tsp salt
2 jalapeños	1tbsp olive oil
3 cloves garlic, chopped	large pinch oregano
	large pinch cumin seeds

1. Roast the green pepper and chillies under a hot grill, in a heavy ungreased frying pan or over an open flame, until they are scorched and charred. Place in a paper or plastic bag or bowl with a tightly fitted lid, and seal. Leave to stand for 30–45 minutes, or until they sweat their skins off. Remove the stalks, seeds and skins, then dice the flesh.
2. Combine the pepper and chillies with the garlic, lime juice, salt and olive oil, then purée. Taste for seasoning and add the oregano and cumin seeds to taste.

NUTRITIONAL INFORMATION			
	TOTAL FAT	SAT FAT	CHOL	ENERGY
Total	12g	2g	0mg	138kcals/575kJ

CHIPOTLES EN ADOBO

CONDIMENT OF SMOKED CHILLIES
IN SWEET-SPICY SAUCE

6 dried chipotle chillies, cut into halves

1 large or 2 medium onions, chopped

6 cloves garlic, chopped

6tbsp cider vinegar or to taste

6tbsp tomato ketchup

2tbsp sugar, preferably dark sugar

pinch salt

450ml/16fl oz water

1tbsp vegetable oil

large pinch each allspice or cloves, cinnamon and cumin

3–4tbsp lime juice or combination of pineapple and lemon juice

1. Place the chipotles in a saucepan with half the onion, 5 cloves of garlic, the vinegar, ketchup, sugar, salt, water, oil and spices.

2. Bring to the boil, then simmer over a low heat for about 20 minutes or until the chillies are softened and the sauce is thickened.

3. Remove the chilli mixture from the heat and add the remaining onion and garlic. Stir in the lime juice and taste for sugar, salt and cloves, adding more to balance the flavour. Leave to cool. Store in the refrigerator for up to a week.

NUTRITIONAL INFORMATION				
	TOTAL FAT	SAT FAT	CHOL	ENERGY
Total	85g	19g	344mg	1520 kcals/6355kJ

CEBOLLAS EN ESCABECHE A LA YUCATECA

PICKLED ONION RINGS
FROM THE YUCATAN

Cebollas en Escabeche are used to garnish nearly everything in the Yucatan. Their tart zing of flavour makes a perfect foil to the sultry flavours of the spicy mixtures of that region: smoky grilled vegetables, spices, seeds and nuts, all ground into complex seasoning pastes.

2–3 red onions, peeled and thinly sliced	juice of 1 orange, plus grated rind of ¼ orange
100ml/4fl oz cider vinegar	50–75ml/2fl oz water
juice of 2 limes	salt to taste
	pinch crumbled dried oregano

1. Combine all the ingredients together. Leave to stand overnight. Chill until ready to use.

NUTRITIONAL INFORMATION				
	TOTAL FAT	SAT FAT	CHOL	ENERGY
Total	85g	19g	344mg	1520 kcals/6355kJ

CHAPTER FIVE

BASICS

★ ★ ★ ★ ★

MEXICAN MAINSTAYS

Whether at home, in restaurants, cafés or street stalls, there are basic dishes that form the makeup of all the others: tortillas, beans and savoury mixtures of tender meats and poultry to be stuffed into antojitos.

TOSTADAS

Stale tortillas make the crispest tostadas as they absorb less oil in the frying.

LOWER FAT TOSTADAS

Brush stale tortillas with vegetable oil and place on a baking sheet in the oven at 220°C/425°F/Gas Mark 7. Bake until golden and lightly browned in places and crisp, about 15 minutes. Alternatively, bake in the oven at 150°C/300°F/Gas Mark 3 for 45 minutes or so. The long slow bake gives a crisper, more brittle crunch to the tostadas. Remove and place on a dry surface.

TRADITIONAL TOSTADAS

Fry the tortillas, one at a time, in shallow vegetable oil or melted lard, until crisp and golden brown. Remove from the pan and drain on absorbent kitchen paper, then place on a dry surface. Keep warm in the oven at 180°C/350°F/Gas Mark 4 for up to 10 minutes: lower the heat to 140°C/275°F/Gas Mark 1 if keeping warm for up to 1 hour.

TOTOPOS (TORTILLA CHIPS)

Cut tortillas into wedges and prepare either in method 1 or 2. Use for chilaquiles, nachos or for tortilla soup.

TORTILLAS DE MAIZ

CORN TORTILLAS

The soft pat, pat, pat of hands slapping against each other flattening out the masa that becomes the tortilla is the traditional background music for the parade of life in much of Mexico.

Modern times have eroded it somewhat: your local taqueria is more likely to have a little machine rolling out the tender flat corn cakes than to have a woman in the kitchen grinding, patting and cooking. But it is still there, sometimes, that elusive comforting sound.

In the city, tortillas are likely to be purchased, or made in the home with a nifty little metal tortilla press. And if the romantic patting sound is sometimes missing, the flavour of the tortillas is still marvellous: earthy, tender corn-scented flat breads, tasting like the essence of Mexican food and like nothing else. Tortillas of course form the basis of much of Mexican cuisine: they are eaten as bread for wrapping up morsels of food, used as utensils for scooping up food, and even as the plate itself, with food placed on top.

MAKES 12 15CM/6IN TORTILLAS
MAKES 24 7.5CM/3IN TORTILLAS

450g/1lb masa flour

175–225ml/6–8fl oz warm room temperature water (less if weather is humid)

several plastic bags, side cut so that each forms a large rectangle

1. Mix the flour with the water until it forms a soft but not sticky dough.

2. Heat a heavy frying pan or comal; I find that using two at a time makes the task quicker and is useful when serving warm tortillas with the meal.

3. Roll a piece of dough into a ball about 4cm/1½in in diameter. Place this ball on one side of a rectangle, then place this onto the open tortilla press. Cover with the other side of the plastic.

4. Close the press and push the handle down evenly and hard. Open up and take the tortilla out of the press – this is easiest to do by picking up the whole press carefully, then peel off the plastic and transfer the tortilla directly into the hot pan. Lightly oiling your hands makes it easier to handle the dough.

If the dough is thick and grainy, it is too dry; if it makes too-fragile tortillas that stick to either the plastic bag or the pan, it is too wet. As the dough tends to dry out as it stands (while you make the other tortillas), you will probably need to add a little more water to the dough, kneading it well as you do.

5. Cook each tortilla quickly, about 2 minutes total. When cooking the first side, wait for the edges to appear dry, then turn over and cook the second side until it is lightly speckled. Turn over and cook the first side a few more moments, then stack on a plate, and keep warm covered with a clean cloth. Tortillas may puff up as they cook; this is a good sign, indicating a light well cooked tortilla. (Some specialities, such as the Yucatecan stuffed tortilla dish, panuchos, are made with tortillas that are especially puffed.)

NUTRITIONAL INFORMATION				
	TOTAL FAT	SAT FAT	CHOL	ENERGY
Total	16.5g	0g	0mg	1840kcals/7700kJ
Per Serving (12)	1g	0g	0mg	153kcals/642kJ
Per Serving (24)	0.5g	0g	0mg	77kcals/321kJ

TORTILLAS DE HARINA

FLOUR TORTILLAS

Flour tortillas, soft flatcakes of wheatflour, are most popular in the northern state of Sonora as they are in the regions that lie north of the border: Arizona and New Mexico.

Wheat was brought here by the cowboys and herders of the Ranchos that covered the area, ground into flour, and rolled out into soft flaccid pancake-like breads rather than puffy, yeast-risen European breads.

Flour tortillas range in size from 10cm/4in to 35 or 50cm/14 or 20in rounds. The larger rounds are stuffed and rolled into burritos and chimichangas.

Note: Lard is the traditional fat used to make flour tortillas. You can buy flour tortillas made with vegetable fat or oil, or even completely fat-free. Wholemeal tortillas, oatbran tortillas, tomato, spinach and other vegetable tortillas can sometimes be found in health food shops.

MAKES 10-12 22CM/9IN TORTILLAS

100g/4oz lard or 100ml/4fl oz vegetable oil	225ml/8fl oz lukewarm water
450g/1lb plain flour, preferably white unbleached, sifted	2tsp salt

1. Work the lard or oil into the flour with your fingers or in a food processor, until it forms a sandy, crumblike mixture.

2. Mix the water and salt, then stir into the flour.

3. Knead the dough for about 3 minutes or until it is no longer sticky. Cover and set aside for at least 2 hours or overnight.

4. Knead the dough again, then roll into small balls. For 18cm/7in tortillas, make 5cm/2in balls, 35cm/14in tortillas will need balls about 75cm/3in in diameter.

5. Place each ball on a floured board, then roll into a 18cm/7in round, paper thin, turning the dough so that the round becomes thin and circular.

6. Heat an ungreased heavy frying pan, griddle or comal. It should be very hot. Place a flat dough round on the hot surface. Leave it for 20–30 seconds – if it puffs up, flatten it again with the back of a spatula.

7. Turn and cook on the other side, only about 10 seconds this time. Stack onto a plate, and keep covered with a clean cloth while you prepare the rest of the dough. The tortillas should be soft and flexible.

8. To use, reheat on the griddle before filling, etc.

NUTRITIONAL INFORMATION				
	TOTAL FAT	SAT FAT	CHOL	ENERGY
Total	130g	51g	116mg	2819kcals/11829kJ
Per Serving (10)	13g	5g	12mg	282kcals/1183kJ
Per Serving (12)	11g	4g	10mg	235kcals/986kJ

REHEATING BOUGHT TORTILLAS, BOTH WHEAT AND CORN MASA

Tortillas should be moist and pliable when reheated. A steamer can do an excellent job, though too much water in the pan and too long cooking can end with sticky results. I prefer the following method, using a lightly oiled frying pan.

1. Lightly spray each tortilla and let them stand a few minutes while you heat a heavy lightly oiled frying pan.

2. Put the whole stack of tortillas in it. When the bottom tortilla is warm, turn the whole stack using a spatula, so that the bottom tortilla is now the top one, or a middle one.

3. Cover and leave to cook in the steam for a few moments, then repeat, dividing the stack of tortillas from the middle. You want each tortilla to be exposed to both heat of the bottom of the pan and the steam that rises to the top.

4. Remove from the pan and place on a plate or in a clean tea cloth, sides folded over to keep the tortillas soft and warm.

FRIJOLES

BEANS

At almost any moment in most any kitchen in Mexico, simmering quietly on a back burner is the earthenware casserole known as "olla", filled with soupy bubbling beans. Such soupy, tender beans, known as frijoles de olla, accompany nearly every meal. They are also ladled into soups, served with meats, puréed and fried then served spread on tortillas for an endless array of tacos, tostadas and enchiladas or enfrijoladas. The liquid from cooking beans is used in soups and stews, and to cook rice. (Arroz negro, rice cooked in black bean liquor is startlingly grey in colour but so very savoury and satisfying to eat.)
The colour, size and shape of your beans depends on where in Mexico you are. In general, black beans are eaten in the Southern more tropical regions, pink and pinto beans further north. However, within this oversimplification there is a huge spectrum of beans and their dishes. White beans, chickpeas, butter beans, yellow beans, all are doted on, added to soups and simmered meals of meats and vegetables.

FRIJOLES REFRITOS

"REFRIED" BEANS

Despite the name "refried", frijoles refritos is not fried twice, rather it is puréed and heated in a small amount of hot fat, more or less fried once. I have heard it said that it is with typical South of the Border exuberance that many things are exaggerated, even the times the beans are fried.

SERVES 6-8

1 recipe pinto, pinquito or other pink beans from Frijoles de Olla (page 77)

1-2 onions, chopped

3tbsp vegetable oil

½tsp ground cumin

½tsp mild chilli powder

salt to taste

1. Mash or purée the beans to obtain a coarse chunky consistency. Leave some whole, some in pieces, others puréed into a thick saucelike mixture.
2. Sauté the onion in the vegetable oil until softened and lightly browned, then sprinkle in the cumin and chilli powder.

3. Ladle in a scoop of the bean mixture. Cook over medium high heat until thickened and slightly darkened in colour. Add another ladleful of the beans and repeat until all the beans have simmered into a thick, darkened, flavourful mixture.
4. Season with salt to taste.

NUTRITIONAL INFORMATION				
	TOTAL FAT	SAT FAT	CHOL	ENERGY
Total	60g	13g	45mg	2347kcals/9914kJ
Per Serving (6)	10g	2g	8mg	391kcals/1652kJ
Per Serving (8)	7.5g	1.5g	6mg	293kcals/1239kJ

VARIATION
FRIJOLES REFRITOS CON QUESO

Top refried pinto or other pink beans with about 175g/6oz grated mild white cheese and either heat in the oven or stir in. Allow the cheese to melt, then serve.

FRIJOLES DE OLLA

SIMMERED BEANS

The green herb epazote, said to help mitigate the embarrassing effects of beans, is usually added to the pot of simmering beans. If unavailable fresh, sometimes it can be found dried. A leaf or two of mint, while not the same thing, gives a similar flavour and result.

Use these beans as an accompaniment to make frijoles refritos, or anywhere it calls for simmered beans. A bowl of warm frijoles de olla, along with a few warm tortillas and a chilli or two is the mainstay of the Mexican diet.

Any of the speckled, most unusual beans such as the earthy, rich Anasazi, are especially delicious cooked this way.

SERVES 6-8

450g/1lb pinto (or pinquito, or pink) or black beans, picked over for stones etc, soaked	1 head of garlic, unpeeled and cut into halves crossways
2 medium onions, chopped	225g/8oz smoky bacon
	3 sprigs of epazote or several leaves of mint
	salt to taste

1. Soak the beans overnight or do a quick soak: place the beans in a saucepan with cold water to cover. Bring to the boil, cook for a few minutes, then remove from the heat. Leave to stand, covered, for an hour. The beans should have plumped up and softened somewhat, absorbing water in the process.

2. Add the onion, garlic, bacon, epazote or mint, and water to the pan.

3. Bring to the boil, then reduce the heat to low and simmer, uncovered, stirring once or twice, for 1½–2 hours or until the beans are softened.

4. Add salt to taste.

NUTRITIONAL INFORMATION

	TOTAL FAT	SAT FAT	CHOL	ENERGY
Total	27g	9g	45mg	2005kcals/8506kJ
Per Serving (6)	4.5g	1.5g	8mg	334kcals/1418kJ
Per Serving (8)	3g	1g	6mg	251kcals/1063kJ

SALSA RANCHERA

COOKED TOMATO SAUCE

This all-purpose tomato and pepper sauce can be used to top eggs for Huevos Rancheros (page 62), served with grilled fish and plantains, thinned with stock for soup. The recipe makes about 2 litres/3½pt and keeps in the refrigerator up to a week, in the freezer for up to 2 months (though it will pale when reheated and needs to be spiced up with chilli pepper upon thawing).

2tsp cumin seeds	2–3 small hot dried chillies, crumbled, or 1 large mild green chilli, such as poblano, roasted, peeled and diced
1.5kg/3lb tomatoes, diced (canned is fine)	
75ml/3fl oz vegetable oil	1 green pepper, roasted, peeled and diced
2–3 small to medium onions, chopped	salt to taste
4–6 cloves, garlic, chopped	2–4tbsp chopped fresh coriander (optional)
1tbsp oregano, crumbled	

1. Toast the cumin seeds until fragrant, then crush coarsely. Set aside.

2. Purée the tomatoes and set aside.

3. Sauté the onions and garlic in the oil until softened, then add the cumin, the oregano, chilli, green pepper and puréed tomatoes.

4. Simmer, stirring often for about 45 minutes or until the sauce is richly flavoured and thickened. Season with salt to taste, adding coriander if using.

NUTRITIONAL INFORMATION

	TOTAL FAT	SAT FAT	CHOL	ENERGY
Total	96g	12.5g	0mg	1162kcals/4833kJ

SALSA DE CHILE PASILLA

MILD RED CHILLI SAUCE

This is the classic red chilli sauce for making enchiladas, or simmering meats, or for spicing up soups or braises. You can omit the tomatoes if you like; or use stock for soaking the chillies for a richer-flavoured sauce.
Add this sauce to browned beef or pork as the braising liquid. Simmer until tender for an excellent chilli rojo con carne, to spoon into bowls or wrap into tortillas for burritos and tacos.

SERVES 4

4 large dried chillies, either all pasilla or half ancho and half pasilla

about 450ml/16fl oz hot but not boiling water or stock

6 cloves garlic, unpeeled

1 onion, peeled

1 clove garlic, chopped

6 ripe tomatoes, quartered (400g/14oz)

¼tsp ground cumin

pinch ground cinnamon

pinch thyme

2–3tsp sugar

salt to taste

1tbsp vegetable oil

juice of ½ lime, plus more if needed to taste

1. Lightly toast the chillies over an open flame or in a heavy ungreased frying pan until they change colour.

2. Remove the stalks, seeds and veins from the chillies. Break up into little pieces and place in a bowl or saucepan. Leave, covered, with a lid, to soften for about 20 minutes. (The liquid should be cool enough to touch and the chillies softened and fleshy.)

3. Meanwhile, roast the whole garlic cloves and onion chunks in an ungreased pan until lightly charred and the garlic is tender. Remove from the heat. When cool enough to handle, remove the skins from the garlic.

4. Chop the garlic and onion and place in a blender with the raw chopped garlic, tomatoes, chillies and enough of the soaking liquid to make a smoothish sauce. When the sauce is smooth, blend in the rest of the soaking liquid and season with cumin, cinnamon, thyme, sugar and salt. (The sauce may be sieved for a smoother, more digestible texture.)

5. Heat the vegetable oil until hot, then ladle in about half of the chilli sauce. Cook down for a few minutes, then ladle in the rest. Cook for about 10 minutes or until the sauce thickens a little and concentrates its flavour.

6. Remove from the heat and season with lime, spices, salt and sugar.

NUTRITIONAL INFORMATION				
	TOTAL FAT	SAT FAT	CHOL	ENERGY
Total	13.5g	2g	0mg	323kcals/1362kJ
Per Serving	3g	0.5g	0mg	81kcals/341kJ

VARIATIONS
USING DIFFERENT CHILLIES

All mild chilli sauces can be prepared this way. For guajillo salsa, use guajillo chillies. Cascabel salsa, use cascabel chillies. Chillies such as ancho, negro, mulatto and some pasillas, will give a dark, almost chocolatey sauce. Light red chillies, such as New Mexico, California, guajillo and some pasilla, will give a brighter lighter red coloured sauce with a lighter, brighter flavour.

MEAT AND POULTRY FILLINGS

Any chilli-scented Mexican spiced mixture makes an excellent filling for tacos, tostadas, burritos and the like. Leftover barbecued chicken or fish, pieces of braised ancho-seasoned pot roast, shreds of meat left over from a braised dinner. All of these make delicious antojito fillings.

CARNE PARA TACOS
SIMMERED PORK FILLING

SERVES 4

1kg/2lb boneless pork, with a little fat for flavour, cut into large bite-sized chunks	1 onion, coarsely chopped
	2 cloves garlic, whole and peeled
any bones cut from the joint	salt and pepper to taste

1. Place the meat in a saucepan with the bones, onion, garlic, salt and pepper.

2. Add cold water to reach the top of the pan. Bring to the boil, then lower the heat and simmer over a very low heat until the meat is just tender, about 1 hour. Remove from the heat and leave the meat to cool in its stock.

3. Take the meat from the stock (save the stock for soup). Shred the meat with a fork and taste for salt and pepper. Warm or brown as desired.

NUTRITIONAL INFORMATION				
	TOTAL FAT	SAT FAT	CHOL	ENERGY
Total	71g	25g	690mg	1512kcals/6325kJ

VARIATIONS
CARNITAS

Add ¼tsp oregano to the meat and add just enough water to cover the meat but no more. Simmer uncovered until the meat is tender and liquid has evaporated. The meat should begin to brown as the liquid reduces and the fat from the meat is rendered out. Continue cooking as the meat browns; turn occasionally and sprinkle with a pinch of cumin as it cooks. Season with salt and pepper to taste and cook until the meat is very tender and nicely browned. This is easily done in the oven as well, instead of the top of the cooker.

CARNE DE RES PARA TACOS (BEEF FILLING)

In place of pork in the above recipe use beef, choosing a cut that has enough fat to encourage browning. If using a lean cut of beef, brown it in a nonstick frying pan with a tiny amount of olive oil to encourage a crusty brown result.

POLLO DESHEBBRADO
SIMMERED CHICKEN

This makes a basic poached chicken that can be used for tacos, tostadas and salads. The cooking liquid makes excellent stock.

SERVES 4

1 chicken, about 1.5kg/3lb	1 onion, chopped
chicken stock to cover (or water mixed with a stock cube or two)	large pinch oregano
	salt and pepper to taste

1. Combine all the ingredients in a saucepan and bring to the boil. Reduce the heat and simmer over a very low heat for 1 hour and 20 minutes or until chicken is just cooked through.

2. Leave the chicken to cool in its liquid, then remove from the pan (saving the delicious liquid for soup or sauce). Dice or pull apart the meat with your fingers.

3. Season with salt and pepper to taste.

NUTRITIONAL INFORMATION				
	TOTAL FAT	SAT FAT	CHOL	ENERGY
Total	45g	13g	630mg	1250kcals/5262kJ

INDEX

Index compiled by Sheila Seacroft